MW00876725

To my friend

Andy Hermansen

Jim Skalire

GOD'S UNBREAKABLE
BLOOD COVENANT
OF
REDEMPTION

Timothy C. Meline & Mike Ahmed

A&M Publishing
Des Moines, Iowa
Copyright © 2018

Copyright © 2018 by Timothy C. Meline and Mike Ahmed

All rights reserved. No part of this book may be reproduced or
transmitted in any form or by any means, electronic or mechanical,
including photocopying, recording or by any information storage and
retrieval system without permission in writing from the publisher.

A&M Publishing
Des Moines, IA 50321
tmeline100@aol.com

Printed in the United States of America

Cover and Chapter Head Design by William Love

Book Design by WORD**ART**, LLC West Des Moines, IA

TABLE OF CONTENTS

PREFACE

Like a masterfully painted portrait, the combined hues of the Old Testament biblical covenants and the celebrated Hebrew feasts, portray the image of Jesus Christ. God's vibrant covenants include those made in the Garden of Eden with Adam, and later with Noah. More of them were made with the patriarchs, Abraham, Isaac, and Jacob (Israel). Jacob's twelve sons became the progenitors of the twelve tribes of Israel, and one of his sons, Joseph, typified Christ in his life and service. After Joseph, additional covenants were made with Moses, and Moses' protégé, Joshua.

Through Moses, God gave His people a myriad of rules and laws. Also, God designed an earthly tabernacle where they could fellowship together on earth. For temple worship, God ordained an earthly priesthood and fashioned a sacrificial system to cover the peoples' sins. In addition, God created ceremonial feasts for the Israelites to keep. As described in the 23rd chapter of Leviticus, the first feast to be celebrated was known as Passover. This feast commemorated the Jewish nation's liberation from slavery in ancient Egypt. Passover was followed by six more feasts, the Feast of Unleavened Bread, First Fruits, Wave Loaves, Trumpets, Day of Atonement, and the Feast of Tabernacles. In different ways, each of these feasts typified the future work of Jesus at His advent.

Other important Old Testament covenants were made between individuals as well as nations. Of particular significance were the covenants made between David and Prince Jonathan. Jonathan's exchange of regal attire with David, and David's keeping of a covenant promise after Jonathan's death, shed light on the covenant ceremony and its austere adherence. Noteworthy, too, are the salt covenants mentioned in the Old Testament. During biblical times, blood and salt were symbolically interchanged. Salt is an incorruptible preservative, and like blood, it, too, is necessary to sustain life.

All of these Old Testament covenants and celebrated feasts beautifully illustrate God's unimaginable love, grace, and mercy through Jesus Christ.

ACKNOWLEDGMENTS

To Dr. Richard Booker, author of *The Miracle of the Scarlet Thread*, and to Malcom Smith, author of *The Power of the Blood Covenant*. Their research and understandings inspired us to write this book. Scripture quotations were taken from the King James Version and New International Versions of the Bible. And a big thank you to our manuscript reviewers for their suggestions, editing, and helpful insights.

DEDICATION

This book is dedicated to Lutheran Church of Hope, its pastors, and congregants, whose life-long mission is to *"Reach out to the world around us and share the everlasting love of Jesus Christ."*

ABOUT THE AUTHORS
WITH
"GOD IN MY LIFE"

TIM MELINE

Tim is a retired real estate trainer. He and his wife Chriss have two married daughters with three grandsons. His entire family are active members of Lutheran Church of Hope in West Des Moines, Iowa. He is actively involved in homeless ministries, and has spent many years sponsoring several Lost Boys from South Sudan. Tim enjoys fishing, photography, and is a published author. He wrote a biography about a South Vietnamese intelligence officer in *Island Detour*; a biographical sketch of 21 people involved in today's mission field titled, *Fishers of Men*; and co-authored a book with one of his Sudanese boys titled, *The Phoenix of South Sudan*. Tim's e-mail address is *tmeline100@aol.com*.

MIKE AHMED

Mike Ahmed was born and raised in Cairo, Egypt. As a young man, he traveled to the United States and converted from his Muslim heritage to Christianity. In the United States he attended a Bible college to become a pastor. After practicing for several years, Pastor Ahmed felt God's call to travel across the United States, and abroad, with the blood covenant message. Mike is a faithful member of Lutheran Church of Hope in West Des Moines, Iowa. He is married and has four grown daughters. He studied and obtained his pilot's license and is certified to scuba dive in deep waters. For speaking engagements, Mike Ahmed can be contacted at barco4Christ@hotmail.com

Additional Insights

The Bible was written by inspired men living in the Middle East. Therefore, in order to grasp the concept of covenant making, an understanding from that cultural mindset is critically important. Mike Ahmed's Middle Eastern background provides legitimacy to the insights presented in this book. To better understand this perspective, an autobiographical sketch of Mike Ahmed's life follows.

GOD IN MY LIFE

By Mike Ahmed

For whatever reason, God decided to lay out a spiritual path for me to follow. I was born into a Muslim family with a younger brother and sister. We were raised in Heliopolis, Egypt, a suburb of Cairo. My birth name was Mohammad Ali Ahmed. Our family was well educated and my mother's ancestors were distant descendants from the Ottoman Empire. We were taught to respect our elders and to place a high priority on education. I attended elementary school in Heliopolis and was taught Arabic. And like all students I memorized parts of the Quran. Five times each day we observed the call to prayer. As a family we worshipped at a mosque and listened to clerics who trained us in Muslim doctrine and the law of Islam.

In 1967, I was in 6th grade when Egypt came under attack from the Israeli Air Force. As a boy I remember hearing air raid speakers, and when evening came my mother turned off all of our lights. At night she shielded a small light so I could do my homework. The bombings were frightening and the memories of those days still linger.

During junior high, my test scores identified an aptitude for math and physics. So I was directed to a high school where those two subjects were emphasized. Besides studying, I really enjoyed playing soccer and while attending high school I worked in an ammunition factory. After graduating from high school, I attended the El Zagazig University. There I studied engineering and earned an industrial diploma in Energy Conservation.

During my college days, I got a job working as a host at the Country Club in Giza. Giza is a suburb located west of Cairo, home of the pyramids. The President of Egypt, Anwar Sadat, was a regular at the Country Club, and we became acquainted. Sadat ruled Egypt from 1970 until 1981, and twice under his predecessor, Gamal Abdel Nasser, Sadat served as Vice President. During the Yom Kippur War of 1973, President Sadat increased in popularity with the Egyptian people. During that battle, the Sinai Peninsula was regained from Israel who had occupied the territory since the Six-Day War in 1967. Afterwards, in 1979, Anwar Sadat engaged Israel's Prime Minister, Menachem Begin, in negotiating the only Egypt-Israeli Peace Treaty in world history. Though generally favorable among the Egyptian people, the Arab world was offended by the Treaty. Yasser Arafat, the leader of the PLO (Palestine Liberation Organization) was livid. What infuriated Arafat's radical Muslim group was a comment made by Sadat stating that the Egyptians didn't have a quarrel with Israel.

The Pharaohs of Egypt were descendants of Noah's son, Ham, while the Arabs were descendants of Noah's son, Shem. Abraham was a descendent Shem and it was Abraham's two sons, half-brothers Isaac and Ismael, who were at odds with each other. So the Pharaohs of Egypt were not a part of Abraham's dysfunctional family tree. Accordingly, Anwar Sadat sought peace between the two countries. Militant Arabs were furious, but to Sadat, peace, not war, made the most sense. Unfortunately, Sadat's actions had consequences. In that same year, Egypt was suspended from the Arab League of Nations, and next to the junior high school I had attended, an Islamic extremist detonated a car bomb. A friend of mine was killed. Two years later, a despicable act by members of an Egyptian Islamic Jihad radically changed my life's path.

On October 6, 1981 I was invited by a friend of mine to attend a ceremony and be seated next to our President, Anwar Sadat. It was something I was really looking forward to attending. Standing in solidarity with our President was quite an honor. But Allah had other plans. My friend's father was a high ranking military official and the person responsible for organizing and hosting a parade. The event commemorated the eighth anniversary of Egypt's crossing the Suez Canal and taking back control of land occupied by the Israelis during the Six-Day War. On the day of the actual ceremony my friend's father was on a pilgrimage to Mecca, and therefore, unable to attend. On his behalf, his son Hesham and I were invited to attend. A military limousine was scheduled to pick us up at my home in Heliopolis. The limo ran late and when it finally arrived, for some unknown reason to me, my body wouldn't allow me to move. The driver said we had to go, so I waived Hesham on and watched as the limo sped away. Later, I learned that Hesham never reached the venue.

On that day, President Sadat and his party were in the stands viewing a procession of military vehicles. Unbeknownst to Sadat and his entourage, Egyptian supersonic jet fighters flew overhead as a deceitful distraction, allowing assassins to slither out of an Egyptian military truck. Under the pretense of saluting, the Egyptian dressed militia approached the Presidential party. Sadat stood to return their salute, and literally, his protective detail "let their guard down." An initial hand grenade was tossed but didn't explode. But then two more were tossed, exploding next to the bewildered President. Then the assassins began firing their AK-47s indiscriminately into the crowd. A designated assassin adjusted his aim and fired directly at Anwar Sadat. Sadat and eleven of his staff were mortally wounded. Another 38 people sustained injuries. Sadat's Vice President, Hosni Mubarak, was standing in the stands but wasn't harmed. A few weeks later, Hosni Mubarak was appointed Egypt's new President.

I became aware of Anwar's death as his assassination flashed across the air waves in Cairo. All of Egypt went into mourning as our 62-year-old martyred President was laid to rest. An inscription was placed on his grave marker, "Hero of War and Peace." I, along with literally thousands of other Egyptians, attended a vast outdoor processional. His casket traveled from a nearby Mosque to the cemetery. As a Muslim, I felt I should have been standing by Sadat's side and killed, too. By not being killed, I felt excluded.

Dying the death of a martyr was esteemed and considered a holy death. According to the cleric's teachings, the shedding of one's blood for an honorable cause absolved one's sins, by-passing hell, and entering heaven. In the Muslim world, clerics taught that a person's sins prevented them from wholeheartedly serving God. And after a person died, they had to spend some time in hell as penance for their sins. I was taught that during life a person wore invisible scales on their shoulders. One scale was weighted down with good deeds while the other scale held one's sins. The sins always outweighed the good deeds, and therefore, sometime in hell was inevitable. However, once a person's sins were absolved in hell, he or she would ascend to heaven. The unsubstantiated teachings made living dreadful. Fear, not faith, resided in your heart. To escape hell, extremists brainwashed those who would listen. Islamic lore established that should a person die as a martyr, their own blood would atone for their sins, and in heaven they would be given a myriad of virgins. Also, if one of its faithful killed a Jew, they were assured of safe passage to heaven. Ironically, the sin(s) of a Muslim did kill a Jew, Jesus. For clarity, the collective sins of all mankind killed Jesus; Muslim, Jew and Christian alike. And because of Jesus' death, the assurance of heaven became possible for "whosoever" would believe in Him.

President Sadat's assassination was a turning point in my life. The tragic display of hatred by the Islamic jihadist caused me to question my belief system. I wondered, "How could any Islamic tenets justify killing such a wonderful man?" My mind ruminated on the extremist's world of violence, compared to the virtues of peaceful co-existence. Later I would come to understand that the Holy Ghost was working on my heart.

Clerics in the mosque talked a lot about hell, but no cleric ever shared with me what it would be like to enter the gates of hell. However, God did! I intervened once to break up a domestic fight. During the altercation, my right hand went flying through a window. The glass broke and a jagged edge severed an artery in my right wrist. Blood began pulsating out of my arm in large quantities. I was rushed to a hospital where the Emergency Room doctors treated me. I had lost a tremendous amount of blood and while lying on the hospital bed my pulse stopped. I lost consciousness and the attending physician pronounced me dead. My soul journeyed to a deep, dark abyss, suspended in total emptiness. Gripped in fear and adrift in this gloomy chasm, I was terrified beyond imagination. In the pitch black space, I couldn't see anyone or anything. But I heard torturous cries filled with deep agony and utter despair. Surging up from the deep, invading my nostrils, were decaying and putrid odors of death and disease. The stench was over-powering and nause-ating. Panic engulfed me and I trembled with fear. Obviously, this vacuum of utter desolation and hopelessness wasn't heaven. It was devoid of any light and appeared as though I had entered the very gates of hell. I pleaded and begged with Allah, "Give me another chance! Please, give me another chance!" As I teetered between the worlds of the living and the dead, my soul ushered back into my body. Like the Genesis account of God breathing air into the nostrils of Adam to give him life, I felt the presence of Allah's breath. It was like a rush of water invading my nostrils and it made me feel like sneezing. After I was pronounced dead, the entire vision must have taken place in less than a minute. As a sheet was being pulled up over my head, I awakened. Having regained consciousness, I lightly touched an attending nurse's hand who was standing next to my bed. She gasped and called for the doctor. In amazement, the doctor pulled the sheet down from my covered face, and asked, "Where did you come from?" Feeling extremely grateful for being alive, I just smiled, deciding to keep quiet about my out-of-body experience. But afterwards I began an exhaustive effort to know God, and in a deep, personal way.

Disenchanted with the demonic mind set of the Islamic jihadist, I obtained a visa and left Egypt in search of a new life. I decided to live in Los Angeles, California. There I found employment at a gas station working as a mechanic. Its owner was an Egyptian. I began studying English but at work spoke mostly in Arabic.

To further my education, I enrolled in Los Angeles' Pierce College. While attending Pierce College, a rather significant event took place. I was driving through Canoga Park, and by divine appointment, came upon a lady standing near a stranded automobile. I stopped to assist her. We exchanged names and she invited me to attend a Bible study in her home. She gave me the time of the study and her address. After giving her invitation some thought, I decided to attend. I drove to her home and when I arrived, several people were already present. The people there asked me about my religion, and for some time we talked about the tenets of my Muslim faith. Then they shared their belief in Jesus and what he did on the cross to atone for sin. I saw that they were living with joy. Eventually I told the group, "If God is powerful, He will convert me to Christianity." Mystifyingly, during our conversation a sensation came over me much like a trance. I felt very much at peace and in my mind distinctly heard words from a book I had yet to read.

Behold, I stand at the door and knock. If anyone hears my voice and opens the door, I will come in to him and eat with him, and he with me.

The voice was full of love and it penetrated deeply into my heart. At that moment I felt engulfed in God's love and His acceptance. I asked, "How do I open the door?" And the reply was simple. *"By believing in your heart and confessing with your mouth that Jesus is Lord. And that God raised him from the dead."* So I did. Without ever opening a Bible, I accepted Jesus as my Lord and Savior. I traded my religion for a relationship and that changed my whole life.

I asked the group to baptize me, and not just sprinkled but immersed. I wasn't vaguely familiar with Christianity or water baptism, but those were the words I spoke. We went into the back yard where there was a swimming pool and I was immersed. To further my understanding of the Bible, a man from the group offered to stop by the garage where I was working and tutor me. He did and my faith grew.

I had one semester remaining at Pierce College when the Spartan College of Aeronautics and Technology in Tulsa, Oklahoma, recruited me away. I accepted the college's invitation and left Pierce without graduating. Many of their entry level students lacked the basic knowledge of math and physics. So, because of my in-depth knowledge of both subjects, I was asked to tutor. It was a paid position and I welcomed the income.

While at Spartan, I befriended a colleague named Michael Joseph. We enjoyed discussing spiritual topics, including the baptism of the Holy Ghost. One evening, while discussing a spiritual matter in a nearby park, I opened my Bible to Isaiah 19. I looked at Verse 18 and was startled to see the name of my hometown. I read the passage, *"In that day (Christ's return) five of Egypt's cities will follow the Lord of Heaven's Armies. They will even begin to speak Hebrew, the language of Canaan. One of these cities will be Heliopolis, the City of the Sun."* Seeing the name of Heliopolis stirred at my soul, and at that moment, I felt God's possible call, nudging me back to Egypt.

After my conversion to Christianity I telephone my mother back in Heliopolis. As expected, she was disappointed with my decision. In fact my family sent a close friend, a high ranking police official, to Tulsa. He asked me to remain faithful to my Islamic roots. Respectfully, I dismissed his request and instead shared with him the gospel of Jesus Christ. I wasn't about to renounce the faith that had just freed me from Islam's legalistic grip. Half-jokingly, my friend said that if I didn't recant, Sharia law required that as an infidel, I be killed. I told him that was foolishness. At that interval, my friend conceded. We said our goodbyes and he returned to Cairo.

When I was close to finishing my courses at Spartan College, I fell asleep one night and had a peculiar dream. I saw myself standing in an admissions office staring at the word Rhema. When I awoke, I searched out the name and found a Rhema Bible College in Tulsa. Believing it to be a sign from God, I decided to enroll.

I drove to the college and was informed by its administrative staff that it was the last day to register. And that was problematic. The application required letters of recommendation from pastors, and an assortment of other requirements, all of which I didn't have time to obtain. Regardless, I told them I'd fill out what I could, leaving the rest blank. I wrote on the application that I had just recently accepted Jesus as my Lord and Savior. And that I had dreamt about registering and was stepping out in faith. I wrote that I didn't know any pastors and was submitting my application without any recommendations. I signed my name and left the application with the administration office.

Later that same day, a friend came up to me at a restaurant and gave me a check. I asked why he was giving me the check and he said, "The Holy Spirit asked me to give it to you to help finance your registration into Bible school." I was dumbfounded, telling him that I had indeed enrolled but wasn't eligible. There were requirements I couldn't meet. But my friend said, "Obviously, God has other plans." That night my phone rang. The Rhema School's secretary called and asked to speak with me. She told me the school's director read my application and accepted it just the way it was submitted. He believed God wanted me to be in that class, and via an Executive Order, I was registered. At that time I adopted the Christian name of Michael, and started referring to myself as Mike Ahmed.

Knowing my cultural background, my Rhema professor and classmates continually asked me questions about covenant making in the Middle East. While elaborating on the subject, I realized that a deeper understanding of the blood covenant was a key to unlocking the Bible. Their inquiry encouraged me to probe even deeper into the subject. And as I did, I found my own faith increasing. I completed my studies at Rhema and graduated.

Not long after graduating, I dreamt that I was digging for petroleum in several places and found none. Then God said to me, "Look at your hands." When I did, I saw huge amounts of pure oil dripping off my hands. At the time I wasn't sure what God meant. But over time I came to understand that God had blessed me with the gift of laying on of hands. As noted in Mark 16:18 *"… they will lay hands on the sick, and they will recover."*

While in Tulsa I opened a large body shop called Performance Options. I hired nine mechanics and as a hobby, built race cars and raced them on a quarter-mile track. I had a Ford Mustang Mach 1 and could lap the quarter-mile in 13 seconds. At work one day I received an invitation from Rhema to meet with a Coptic monk who was touring from Egypt. We met during a revival meeting and, point blank, he asked me what I was going to do with the gift God had given me. I asked, "What gift?" He answered, "To set the captives free." His words referenced a passage from Luke 4:18-19, *"The Spirit of the Lord is upon me, because he hath anointed me to preach the gospel to the poor; he hath sent me to heal the brokenhearted, to preach deliverance to the captives, and recovering of sight to the blind, to set at liberty them that are bruised, to preach the acceptable year of the Lord."* I told him that I didn't know. During the service there was a lot of prayer and the laying on of hands.

One of the evangelists at the meeting was from Israel. He was praying and laying hands on people. It appeared they were being healed, but I was skeptical. Later though, I became convinced that the Holy Ghost actually healed those with infirmities. Father Daniel invited me to go to California with him in order to attend the next scheduled revival meetings. I was reluctant to leave my job and family but finally agreed. Before landing in California, we made a stop in St. Louis. In St. Louis, I met an evangelist from Israel who asked me to join him at a different revival meeting in California. I had time to attend both and agreed. During the revival meeting it became apparent from the dream I had about having oil on my hands, that it was indeed a gift from God. I was expected to lay hands on the sick. I attended the healing services with Father Daniel and began laying hands on the sick and lame. The Holy Ghost came upon me and those with infirmities were healed. That ten-day revival period began my ministry.

Fast forward, one day at home in Tulsa, I encountered a life and death situation. Our garage door jammed and I decided to fix it myself. My conscience warned me, "Don't do it," but I went ahead anyway. I began working on a crooked bolt that was intricately attached to the garage door's cable. Bringing my hammer down on the crooked bolt, I swung pretty hard. The cable and spring broke and the bolt's trajectory smacked me between my eyes. Afterwards, I discovered that I had been hit with a six-inch bolt. It ricocheted off of my skull before lodging in some sheetrock inside the garage. The velocity was intense and I suffered a concussion. From the impact I saw bright lights and heard my inner voice telling me, "get up, don't pass out, and crawl into the house." With the temporary loss of sight in one eye, I crawled from the garage into the house. When I appeared, our three-year-old daughter Sarah saw me and prayed immediately, "Jesus, heal my daddy!" I was rushed to the hospital.

At the hospital I asked for a doctor who had been a classmate at Rhema with me. I was told that he on a mission trip and out of town. My punctured head was x-rayed. Not knowing the exact circumstances behind the accident, the attending physician began looking for a bullet. To everyone's surprise, the following day my doctor friend showed up. He left early because of a spiritual prompting that he might be needed back home. We prayed together.

The x-rays revealed that the bolt had penetrated my skull and came within centimeters of my brain. Fractured bones were floating precariously close to both the brain and sinus cavity. Immediate surgery seemed necessary. But just before the surgery, I requested another x-ray. The attending physician struggled with my request, telling me it was urgent that the surgery be performed. But I was convinced that God was healing me, making surgery unnecessary.

By working on the garage door myself, I was fully aware that I had messed up. Regardless, I was in covenant with God, and by faith I believed He would perform a miracle. The attending doctor was irritated with me but conceded, and an x-ray was ordered. While the x-ray was being examined, the doubting doctor continued preparing me for surgery. I protested and exclaimed, "God healed me!" As the doctor was about to cut into my face a radiologist interrupted the surgeon. He said, "Look at this." My x-rays showed no signs of bone fragmentation. My friend, Dr. Mast, was informed of the new x-ray and announced over the intercom, "There will not be any surgery on Mr. Ahmed." The Great Physician had performed a miracle and Dr. Mast let everyone hear the good news over the hospital's intercom. My little Sarah's prayer had been answered.

After graduating from Rhema, I accepted an internship to pastor at the Living Word Bible Church in North Dakota. I stayed there for a year before accepting an invitation to share a pastorate in St. Charles, Iowa. While pastoring in Iowa, I began teaching on God's covenants with special emphasis on the Covenant of Redemption. I recorded a cassette series titled, *The Blood Covenant* and made speaking appearances across the United States. As an evangelist I appeared on television's Trinity Broadcast Network (TBN).

For a while we lived in Winterset, Iowa. One day, while driving through town, a young boy on a bicycle jumped the curb right in front of my car. I was driving the speed limit but it happened so fast I didn't have time to hit my brakes. His body went up over the bumper and struck the windshield before flying several feet in the air. I stopped the car and ran over to his lifeless body lying on the ground. A neighbor ran to the scene. She was trained as a paramedic and tried to revive the boy's lifeless body. A neighbor began comforting me and said, "Mike, it wasn't your fault. I saw the whole thing. He rode his bike right in front of you." The boy wasn't responding to any lifesaving efforts, so the paramedic backed away from his body. Then I said to myself, "That little boy isn't going to die on my watch!" I knelt down and laid hands on his body. For five minutes I prayed out loud to God. In earnest, I asked God to restore life back into his unresponsive body. As the Holy Ghost fell upon me, I heard the words, "John, arise and walk." By faith I said those words and immediately life came back into his fractured body. Without missing a beat, he stood up and ran home. God was merciful that day and used my anointing to witness to those in earshot of my prayer.

In 1996, I felt prompted by the Holy Ghost to return to Cairo. My passport identified me as Mike Ahmed. Upon arrival at the Cairo International Airport, I handed my passport to the airport security officer. Immediately, I was detained. Unbeknownst to me, a Muslim cleric in America heard my conversion testimony on the radio and reported it the Islamic authorities in Cairo. As a result my name was on an airport blacklist, and

I was about to be arrested. But God rescued me. While being escorted away, I looked up and an assistant to the head of immigration was carrying a sign which read, "Mike Ahmed." I said, "Hey, that's me." The officer holding the sign held a higher rank than the officer detaining me. The officer with the sign sternly ordered the restraining officer to let me go. It was clear that my custody was going to be under his authority and not the person detaining me. The perplexed officer did as he was told and I was ushered to the airport's immigration office. To my surprise, the high ranking officer in charge of immigration was the same family friend who had flown to Tulsa in an attempt to persuade me to renounce my Christianity. Seeing my old friend put me at ease. He told me the names of suspected terrorists and spies were on the airport's blacklist. Then he said, "For some odd reason, I had a feeling you were on that plane from Germany, and that is why I sent my assistant with your name on the sign." My friend told me I was free to go, and said, "Let me know the next time you come, I'll have you escorted, because once your name is on the blacklist, it's never removed." I thanked him profusely and then went about my "underground" missionary business. While in Cairo, I taught a Christian course titled *Alpha* in the homes of new converts.

After returning to America, I was notified that several converts had been arrested on bogus espionage charges. And that their prosecuting attorney was my younger brother, Ahmed. I called and told him the charges were bogus and asked him to be lenient. I knew America's continued financial aid to Egypt carried a caveat, religious freedom. After much prayer, Egypt's government acknowledged America's demand and passed a "religious freedom" law. Therefore, those converting from Islam to Christianity were supposed to be protected from prosecution. My brother asked how I knew so much. I told him that I was a Christian missionary and was the person responsible for their conversion. My words hit a very sensitive chord and he became incensed. These converts had broken their Islamic covenant, and as far as he was concerned, they were going to be punished. He threatened to throw the book at them, even possible execution. Then he told me that their arrest was none of my business and I wasn't to come within a hundred miles of him. I told him he was an unjust judge and that his animosity toward me was clouding his judgment. He retorted self-righteously, "I have been just all my life." I said, "If so, why are you prosecuting people you don't know anything about?" He told me I was wrong. We exchanged some heated words before I challenged him to reach for a Bible and look for the truth. I asked him to recluse himself or I would be forced to go over his head and file an embarrassing conflict of interest complaint. He finally relented and disqualified himself. With a new prosecutor, the harassed converts were given a light sentence and eventually released.

On another occasion Ahmed was forced to work with me on some family business. My mother's ancestors were once members of a royal family. However, when she was very young a foreign government reigned in Egypt. That government took hold of her family's wealth and property along the Nile River. When

Anwar Sadat came into power he began restoring the rights to property owners whose property was unlawfully confiscated. A restoration paper concerning her family's property was discovered and being the oldest son it was my responsibility to determine its content. As a result, my brother had to sit down with me and talk. Unannounced, I arrived at his office with a pastor friend of mine from the United States. I advised the pastor not to speak much about Jesus to my brother. We went to a restaurant to break bread and talk. Eating a meal together meant a lot because if we were enemies that wouldn't happen. In the Middle East men are either friends or enemies. We don't have acquaintances. You are either all in, or all out; gray areas don't exist. Why share a meal or sit at a table with someone who one day might be betray you? So having lunch together was a big deal.

While eating, my brother inquired about my friend and I told him he was a pastor. I told my brother that just prior to leaving for Cairo, my pastor friend had an interesting dream that he dreamt twice. In his dream he saw a young man with dark, thick hair calling him for help. The man was in a room with marble floors, sitting on a head table defending someone. Then I said to my brother, "He wants to know if it was you?" My brother just listened. Later that same day I went alone to my brother's office. When I approached him, he seemed troubled. Then he told me that he had the identical vision as my pastor friend, only he had dreamt it five times. He didn't want to discuss it but I knew that the Holy Spirit was working on my brother's heart. And that same Holy Spirit guides my heart.

In conclusion, I am most grateful for my Egyptian heritage because it has enriched my cultural understanding of the Middle East. Insights and perspectives from these cultural eyes are shared throughout this narrative. Hopefully, any challenging insights will be buffered by knowing some of my background.

God In My Life is a testimony to the transformation power of the Holy Ghost and the authority imparted to God's children. As written in 1 John 4:4,"Greater is he that is in you, than he that is in the world."

The End

For the life of the flesh is in the blood:
and I have given it to you upon the altar
to make an atonement for your souls:
for it is the blood that makes
an atonement for the soul.

Leviticus 17:11

GLOSSARY

To enhance understanding several foreign words and/or phrases used in this book have been alphabetically listed and defined.

Adamic Covenant - Adam was made in the image of God and given authority to reign over a garden paradise. God loved Adam and made for him a wife. In return for all of this blessing, Adam was expected to be obedient. God told him not to eat the fruit from one specific tree. This initial conditional covenant with Adam was called the Edenic Covenant. But Adam disobeyed, introducing sin into God's perfect garden paradise. And Adam's sin had consequences. Several curses were instituted against Adam and Eve, including inescapable physical death. However, while the consequences of their sins were severe, out of divine love, God added a supporting covenant of grace known as the Adamic Covenant or Covenant of Redemption.

Agape – Agape is a Greek word describing divine love at its zenith. It is different from brotherly love or Eros which is a sexual type of love. It can best be described as the voluntary, sacrificial kind of love displayed by Jesus on the cross at Calvary.

Atonement – This is God's method for forgiving sin in order for mankind to restore his broken fellowship with God. In the Old Testament animal sacrifices were used to cover the people's sins without actually removing them. In the New Testament, Jesus' death on the cross at Calvary completely atoned for mankind's sins (past, present, and future).

Circumcision – This is the surgical removal of a male child's foreskin. In God's covenant with Abraham, circumcision became a religious rite, identifying the Hebrew people as His own. However, in the New Testament, Christians were not required to observe this external rite. References to circumcision in the New Testament are made concerning the heart. For example, we read in Colossians 2:9, *"or in him dwelled all the fullness of the Godhead bodily. And ye are complete in him, which is the head of all principality and power: In whom also ye are circumcised with the circumcision made without hands, in putting off the body of the sins of the flesh by the circumcision of Christ: Buried with him in baptism, wherein also ye are risen with him through the faith of the operation of God, who hath raised him from the dead."* So today, the circumcision of the heart, not the flesh, allows believers to honor the Lord with all their heart and soul.

Contextualization is a Christian mission word that refers to presenting the gospel message in a way that is relevant to a particular culture. Rather than asking the people of a particular ethnic group to commit cultural suicide, contextualization utilizes their culturally relevant ways to present the gospel.

Covenant – Biblical covenants were essentially legally binding promises given by one party to another. Some promises were unconditional, while other promises had conditions and specified consequences for breaking covenant.

Cutting Covenant – This phrase gives reference to a covenant ceremony where an animal is cut or divided into two parts. Animal halves are placed on the ground and the parties making covenant stand or walk through the halves. By doing so, the parties are ritually dying to themselves in order to live for the other party.

Hematidrosis – A medical term referring to the sweating of blood. It is a rare condition where perspiration becomes mixed with a person's blood. Its occurrence takes place in times of great physical or emotional stress like the trauma Jesus experienced in the Garden of Gethsemane.

Jehovah-Jireh – This is the name of the place where God provided Abraham with a substitute ram as a burnt offering unto Him instead of Isaac. It means God is your provider.

Pre-incarnate Son of God – As revealed in the Trinity, this phrase identifies Jesus Christ as His eternal deity. In the Old Testament Christ appeared many times in His pre-incarnate state. Interestingly, if Christ did not exist prior to His incarnation, then He cannot be God. The Trinty is mentioned in Genesis 1:26 when God said, *"Let Us make man in Our likeness."*

Second Advent or **Second Coming** refers to the Christian belief of Jesus' future return as King of Kings and Lord of Lords.

Shekinah – This Hebrew word describes any place where God's divine presence and glory dwells. God's Shekiah glory appeared as God lead the Israelites on their wilderness journey out of Egypt. And it appeared in the Holy of Holies, filling the Tabernacle Temple with intense light.

Showbread - Inside the Israelites earthly "tent" tabernacle, showbread was baked and placed on specific table. Each week, twelve loaves of bread baked with fine flour, were prepared by temple priests. The baked loaves were placed on a designated table inside the Holy Place. And they remained there, in the presence of the Lord, during the entire week. On the Sabbath day the loaves were removed and eaten by the priests before new loaves were set out. It was God's invitation for a "meal" of fellowship with His people via God's earthly priests.

The showbread typified Christ. In John 6:35, 49-50, Jesus said, *"I am the bread of life. He who comes to me will never go hungry, and he who believes in me will never be thirsty. Your forefathers ate the manna in the desert, yet they died. But here is the bread that comes down from heaven, which a man may eat and not die."* And during Jesus' last Passover meal, He took bread, gave thanks and broke it, and gave it to his disciples, saying, *"Take and eat; this is my body."*

Transubstantiation – While maintaining their actual appearances, the Eucharist elements of bread and wine become the actual body and blood of Christ. Believing this places a high regard on receiving communion.

INTRODUCTION

To discover how blood covenants were created during Old Testament times, imagine living in an Israeli community. Now allow your imagination to observe the actions of two Hebrew men initiating a blood covenant. Initially, the men exchange their outer robes. Symbolically the exchange is a promise to care for one another. Then the belts that hold their weapons are removed and exchanged. In essence, they are vowing to one another all of their support and protection. In other words, should either come under attack, the other person is agreeing to fight alongside them. And if required, to shed their own blood for the other person's sake. After the exchange of belts, an animal's throat is cut and its body separated down the middle. The sacrificed halves represent each person dying to himself on the other person's behalf. The bloody halves are laid on the ground and separated. The two men then stand with their backs to each other between the separated halves. Then starting with their backs to each other, the two men parade around each half in a figure eight pattern, arriving back to the middle, only this time facing each other. The palms of their right hands are cut, and with right arms raised, their blood is intermingled.

Next, before witnesses, the two men read off their assets and liabilities. By agreement they are saying, "All that is mine is yours, including my debts, and all that is yours is mine. And if I should die, by adoption, all of my children are yours, and you will become responsible for my entire family's well-being." And vice-versa.

The ceremony concludes with a covenant meal. A loaf of bread is broken with each man feeding a piece of that bread into the mouth of the other. Wine is served and shared the same way. The bread is symbolic of their bodies being put inside each other, and the wine, the merging of their life-giving blood. By this ceremony, the two men become blood brothers.

As a memorial, a tree is sprinkled with the sacrificed animal's blood and planted. After the ceremony each man adopts the other person's last name as a part of their new covenant name. From that day forward they are known by the highest honor one could ever have in the Middle East; they are known as friends. A word which isn't spoken lightly. Knowing this, we should have a deeper appreciation for the passage in John 15:15. Jesus said, "Henceforth I call you not servants; for the servant knoweth not what his lord doeth: but I have called you friends; for all things that I have heard of my Father I have made known unto you." By referring to His disciples as "friends," Jesus was paying them, and subsequently all Christians, a tremendous honor.

Afterwards, the resulting scars serve as reminders of their covenant bond and all accompanying responsibilities.

Covenant Adherance

For an introductory understanding of the serious nature of covenant adherence, imagine another scenario. Our fictitious account takes place in an Egyptian neighborhood. This portrayal is graphic and meant to illustrate the black and white elements of covenant keeping. While the storyline is meant to be fictional, it isn't far from reality. Though strict covenant observance is rare in Western society, Middle Eastern cultures treat them with utmost respect.

Our story involves a thirteen-year old boy named Paki and a neighborhood boy named Zahur. Paki and Zahur attend the same all boys school. The boys live in a village near the town of Luxor, Egypt. Both boys find themselves attracted to the same girl. She is a very pretty Egyptian girl named Myrrh. Myrrh attends an all girl school just a couple of blocks away from their school.

Myrrh is Paki's love interest. Zahur finds her attractive too and makes an overture by walking to her home to visit. Paki sees Zahur visiting with Myrrh and a spirit of jealousy invades his heart.

On the way home from school one day, Paki decided to hurt Zahur. He picked up a large rock and hid behind a tree. Knowing Zahur walked home that same way, he waited patiently in the shadows. Paki was going to teach Zahur a lesson. He watched covertly as Zahur approached. Unsuspectingly, Paki slipped up behind him and bashed his head with the rock. Zahur let out a shriek just before falling in deathly silence to the ground. A neighbor woman heard Zahur's cry and came hurriedly out of her home. She rushed to his aid and called for medical attention. The injured boy was taken to a nearby clinic where he was pronounced dead.

The boys' fathers, Magdi and Menkera, were blood brothers. Many years before, using a razor blade, each man made a fairly deep incision in his wrist. With blood oozing out, their wrists were tightly tied together and their blood freely mingled. On a table in front of them was a loaf of bread and two glasses filled with wine. The men released their tie and dropped some of their blood into the other man's glass. The blood was stirred as each man drank from their glass. Pieces of bread were torn and fed to one another. During the ceremony the men exchanged a series of promises including an exchange of all assets and liabilities. In other words, "all that is mine is yours, and all that is yours is mine. And should you become unable to care for your children, I will become a father to them and care for them. And should you become ill and die, I will take care of your family." And vice-versa. Another promise stated, "If anyone from my family should ever take the life of anyone in your family, you can take that child in exchange. And it will be your prerogative to either care for the exchanged child as a member of your family; or accepted as a slave; or yours to slay (an eye for an eye)." The pact was sealed in their blood, never to be broken, and the men became known as friends.[1]

[1] Neither in the Arabic or Hebrew language is there a corresponding word for "acquaintance." In the Middle East, men either have friends or enemies. And you cannot be a friend unless you are in covenant with someone. So, if you are not in covenant, you are considered an enemy. A part of the covenant ceremony included each partner identifying the other with the highest honor, friend.

In this scenario, Paki's life was expected to be exchanged for the taking of Zahur's life. In this most difficult context Paki's father's covenant integrity is tested. Ceremoniously, Paki had to be escorted to Zahur's father's house. And once he arrived, Paki's fate was in Zahur's father's hands. That was part of the covenant agreement and it had to be honored by Paki's father.

From inside Paki's home, abysmal groanings reverberated loudly. The haunting noises from inside Paki's house carried out into the street. Previous dialogue between the boy's mother (Sitra) and father (Magdi) brought about the groanings. Their conversations had been intense and passionate. Paki was now being turned over to Magdi's covenant friend, Menkera, and Sitra felt her whole world coming to an end. She was grief-stricken. Sitra's tears were filled with anguish and her contorted facial expressions revealed unfathomable agony. What she felt was cavernous, emotional pain, Her entire body felt grief stricken. In her mind she asked, "What insane bond requires such a reprehensible act as giving up one's son for the life of another?" She begged her husband, "Break your covenant and let us move to Turkey." But Magdi was a man of honor. If he reneged on the blood covenant his family's name would be forever stained. No, with eyes wide open he had entered into a blood covenant with Menkera; and on this day, Magdi would prove he was a man of honor. As Magdi walked Paki out the front door, Sitra's shrill pleading continued, "No! No! No!" Outside of their house, lying on the ground, was an empty pine box. A coffin.

Members of the Paki's extended family picked up the coffin

and began carrying it down the dirt road. Walking in front of the coffin was Paki. His hands were open and held up, holding a burial napkin. Their destination was the home of the dead boy's family. On one side of the road, mourning for Paki, were grieving friends and family. They were crying and tossing dirt over their heads and bodies. The air surrounding them was clouded in dust. On the other side of the road, people appeared jubilant. Reflecting on Magdi's covenant keeping, their praises were of commendation. The procession moved forward until Paki reached the home of the deceased Zahur. The parading stopped. At this juncture, Zahur's father would decide Paki's fate. Not knowing what he would do created much drama.

The father had choices. He could forgive the boy and send him back with his parents. Or he could keep him as a slave in his household. Or he could take Paki's life.

Unemotionally, Zahur's father appeared. In front of the crowded assembly, Menkera pulled out a dagger and slit the boy's throat. Blood gushed out from Paki's neck and within seconds Paki's lifeless body slumped to the ground. His dead body was placed inside the coffin and pall bearers carried Paki's dead body to the cemetery. The boy's death removed the covenant breach between the blood brothers, reinstating their original covenant. This was covenant law. It was serious, never to be taken lightly.

PART ONE

OLD
TESTAMENT
COVENANTS

"AND REDEMPTION BEGINS, WITH A BABY IN BETHLEHEM."

Lyrics from *When Hope Came Down* by Kari Jobe

THE BLOOD COVENANT OF REDEMPTION
(EDENIC AND ADAMIC COVENANTS)

God's Love Story

Revealed throughout the Bible is God's unimaginable love for mankind. The fascination is why? One answer is given to us in I John 4:8 where we read, *"God is love."* The very nature of God is love. And for love to exist it must have someone to whom it can express itself. John 3:16 describes God's love this way, *"For God so loved the world that he gave His only Begotten Son."* This verse describes the very essence of God's love. God so loved all men under heaven that being a Triune God, gave himself as a sacrifice in the form of Jesus. Jesus expanded on the depth of this love by saying, *"Greater love has no one than this: to lay down one's life for one's friends."* The Covenant of Redemption revealed in this first chapter reflects God's enormous love for Adam and all of Adam's descendants.

1

What is man, that thou art mindful of him?

In Genesis 1:14-15 God said, *"Let there be lights in the firmament of the heaven to divide the day from the night; and let them be for signs, and for seasons, and for days, and years: And let them be for lights in the firmament of the heaven to give light upon the earth: and it was so."*

Gazing upon God's celestial creation is overwhelming. The most observable cosmic marvel is our sun. It is 1.3 million times the size of earth and perched some 90+ million miles away. Together with our moon, the eight other primary planets, and myriad of stars, God created the Milky Way Galaxy. The stars themselves are hundreds of thousands of times further away than the sun. And astronomers tell us that beyond our galaxy, billions of light years away, are billions of other galaxies. In other words, God's universe is infinitely large. But the renown of God extends even further than the unfathomable intergalactic universe. His outstretched hand extends to every person on planet earth. The Psalmist (Psalms 8:1, 3-5) was in awe of this fact when he wrote, *"Lord, our Lord, how majestic is your name in all the earth! When I consider your heavens, the work of your fingers, the moon and the stars, which you have set in place, what is mankind that you are mindful of them, human beings that you care for them? You have made them a little lower than the angels and crowned them with glory and honor."* In this Psalm, we acknowledge David's amazement of God's devotion and love for mankind. In Genesis God's covenant relationship with Adam, and subsequently all of mankind, demonstrates the depth of God's sacrificial love.

The Covenants found in Genesis and throughout the Bible

The following chart identifies the various covenants found in the Bible and serves as an outline for the reader.

Covenants of the Bible		
Covenants	**Obligations**	**References**
Edenic Covenant	To procreate and subdue the earth in an eternal, sinless environment. Conditioned on not eating from the Tree of Life. If so, the consequence would be curses and physical death.	Genesis 1: 26-30 Genesis 2:15-17
Adamic Covenant or Blood Covenant of Redemption	God's unconditional promise to send a Redeemer whose blood sacrifice would forgive all sin. And until that time, required blood sacrifices to temporarily cover man's sins.	Genesis 3:15-19
Noahic Covenant	For Noah and his family to repopulate the earth, and God's unconditional promise to never again destroy planet earth by flood.	Genesis 8:20-22 Genesis 9:8-17
Abrahamic Covenant and the Melchizedek Priesthood	An unconditional promise for Abraham's descendants to occupy a distant land. And a promise to be Abraham's God (and all of his descendants), conditioned on every male being circumcised. Abraham met a King from Salem who was also a priest of the Most High. His name was Melchizedek and Abraham paid homage to him. Psalm 110:4 prophesied that the Messiah would be a priest after the same order as Melchizedek.	Genesis 12:1-3; 7 Genesis 14 Genesis 15:6-21 Genesis 17 Psalm 110:4 Hebrews 5,6,7,8
Mosaic/Sinai Covenant	In return for obeying God's commandments, God promised to protect and bless Israel. However, should they became disobedient, God's Mosaic covenant stated that they would be cursed.	Exodus, Chapters 19 – 24 Leviticus 26 Deuteronomy, Chapters 28-29
Aaronic Priesthood	In return for obeying God's commandments, God promised to dwell with His people, and to protect and bless them. And again, if they became disobedient, to expect a curse. God made an everlasting covenant giving Aaron and his Levite descendants, power and authority to act in God's name. This earthly priesthood was assigned the task of dealing with the people's sins. As a	Exodus 28:1-43 Hebrews 7:8,15-16, 23-25

Covenants	Obligations	References
	sinner himself, Aaron was required to offer up sacrifices like everyone else. Only on the Day of Atonement was Aaron allowed to meet with God in the Holy of Holies. When Aaron died another Levite Priest became necessary. The Aaronic priesthood was based on ancestry while the priesthood of Melchizedek was based on everlasting life. After Jesus crucifixion, the veil in the temple was torn. The torn veil was symbolic. God identified that earthly high priests were no longer required to fellowship with God. After His resurrection, Jesus became mankind's intercessor, king, and sinless High Priest.	
Davidic Covenant	God reaffirmed the promise of a homeland made in both the Abrahamic and Mosaic Covenants. God telescoped promises to David foretelling that his name would be great and God made an unconditional promise to institute and establish the royal Davidic house forever. This covenant promise was fulfilled during Jesus' first advent.	2 Samuel 7:5-17 1 Chronicles 17:11-14 2 Chronicles 6:16
Palestinian Covenant	God's unconditional promise to forgive unfaithful Israel; to give them a new heart; to gathering them from the ends of the earth; and to live with Him in the Promised Land.	Deuteronomy 30:1-10 Jeremiah 31:31-34 Ezekiel 36:24-37 Hebrews 8:7-12
New Messianic Covenant	Jesus' first advent and sacrifice introduced a new covenant. This covenant of grace and peace is for those who believe that Jesus' sacrifice atoned for their repentant sins, and promises that in the fullness of time, eternity with the Trinity.	Isaiah 9:6-7 John 3:16 Romans 5:1-2; 12-20 Ephesians 1:1-10 Philippians 4:7 Revelation 22:1-5

The Edenic Covenant

Genesis records that Adam was made in God's image and God's love was lavished on him. God created a garden paradise for Adam, literally a heaven on earth. God filled the garden with magnificent animals, numerous birds, incredible flora life, an abundance of fruit trees, and no doubt, healthy vegetables. God delighted in Adam, delegating all of Eden's gardening responsibilities, as well as naming all of God's created animals. As God's steward, Adam and God were in close fellowship. In Genesis 2:15-17 God told Adam he could eat fruit from any of the abundant trees in God's garden, except one. And that particular tree was located in the middle of the garden. This was a conditional covenant, conditioned on Adam's obedience, and known as the Edenic Covenant.

"The Lord God took the man and put him in the Garden of Eden to work it and take care of it. And the Lord God commanded the man, 'You are free to eat from any tree in the garden; but you must not eat from the tree of the knowledge of good and evil, for when you eat from it you will certainly die.' " With physical death as a consequence, Adam remained obedient, living in harmony with the land and his Creator.

Adam's relationship with God was great, and God made it even better. God didn't want Adam to be alone so God created for him a wife. Adam said poetically of Eve, *"This is now bone of my bones, and flesh of my flesh. She shall be called woman, because she was taken out of man."* Therefore a man shall leave his father and mother and be joined to his wife, and they shall become one flesh. During their sexual union, Adam and Eve became wholly "one flesh."

In Genesis 1:28 we read where *"God blessed them and said, 'Be fruitful and increase in number; fill the earth and subdue it. Rule over the fish in the sea and the birds in the sky and over every living creature that moves on the ground.'"*

Adam's Fall from Grace

Though never stated, it is understood that Adam told Eve about God's command not to eat any fruit from the forbidden tree in the middle of the garden. Sometime later, how long isn't known, Satan disguised himself as a serpent, entered the garden, and engaged Eve in conversation. The serpent encouraged her to doubt the explicit instructions given to Adam. She was enticed to lust after the forbidden fruit and to covet the tree of knowledge. The serpent told Eve, *"If you eat of the forbidden tree you will not die. Instead, your eyes will be opened, and like God, you will know the difference between good and evil."* By telling Eve that she wouldn't die, Eve must have been keenly aware of the penalty assigned to her disobedience. During the moment of temptation she had a choice; she could either obey or disobey God's command. It was freely her choice. Sadly, Eve fell prey to Satan's ruse and ate at his table of deception. After biting into the forbidden fruit, Eve gave the illicit fruit to her husband. First Timothy 2:14 acknowledges that while Eve was deceived, Adam willfully disobeyed. Regardless, both transgressed, and original sin was unleashed into the garden. The power of sin that ensnared them, now enslaved them. With their failed attempt to become equal with God, God's perfect garden paradise became stained.

Original Sin

Adam and Eve had free will. They had the option of being obedient or disobedient. However, the consequences for being disobedient were compulsory not optional. And their rebellious nature brought about negative consequences. What was so wrong with what they did? Their sin was more than just wanting to be like God, it was unwittingly desiring to become God. Their insubordinate behavior demonstrated the desire to remove themselves from any judgment or oversight. And it is the same sin which plagues society today when it says, "we are gods unto ourselves, and nobody is going to tell us what to do, or what's right and what's wrong." Clearly, the sin that ensnared and enslaved Adam and Eve is the same sin which perverts society today.

Besides losing their innocence and their eventual physical death, in Genesis 3:16 God tells Eve, "*I will make your pains in child-bearing very severe; with painful labor you will give birth to children. Your desire will be for your husband, and he will rule over you.*" And to Adam in verses 17-19, God said, "*Because you listened to your wife and ate fruit from the tree about which I commanded you, 'You must not eat from it,' cursed is the ground because of you; through painful toil you will eat food from it all the days of your life. It will produce thorns and thistles for you, and you will eat the plants of the field. By the sweat of your brow you will eat your food until you return to the ground, since from it you were taken; for dust you are and to dust you will return.*"

Genesis 2:9 identifies another tree in the garden called the tree of life. That tree has significance because of another verse found in the Genesis 3:24. And the Lord God said, "*The man has now become like one of us, knowing good and evil. He must not be allowed to reach out his hand and take also from the tree of life and eat, and live forever.*" It appears that the fruit from that tree perpetuated life, and God didn't want Adam and Eve to live in an endless state of sin. So God banished them from the garden and blocked its entrance. Though their waywardness alienated them from the perfect relationship they once enjoyed, their sin never diminish God's love for them. God designed a way for them to stay in fellowship.

When God created Adam, and subsequently Eve, God didn't impose His will on them. It was their moral responsibility to be obedient. God gave Adam and Eve the autonomy to choose right from wrong. Without choice, Adam and Eve would have been nothing more than programmable humanoids. Both of them were keenly aware that the tree of knowledge was off limits. That tree probably wasn't much different than any of the other fruit trees, except their decision to eat of it was spiritually deadly. Biting into the fruit opened their eyes to the "*knowledge of good and evil.*" Recognizing their nakedness they covered themselves with fig leaves. So instead of running to God, seeking forgiveness, they ran away and hid themselves.

Sin and Death

Adam's inability to remain obedient produced dire

consequences. His sin left mankind in a fallen state of separation from the holiness of God. Mercifully, God designed a redemptive way to restore their fellowship. To cover Adam and Eve's nakedness God fashioned clothing out of animal skins. God allowed an animal's shed blood to cover, without actually removing, their intentional sin. This animal sacrifice foreshadowed in time an ultimate blood sacrifice which would permanently atone for all of mankind's sins.

God might have explained it to them this way. "Adam and Eve, for the time being, if you accept this animal sacrifice as a covering for your sins, it will restore our fellowship. However, in order for me to continue seeing you as righteous, it will be necessary for you to continue offering animal sacrifices." By inference, God's arrangement for covering their sins was to be taught and passed on to their children. And from their children to their children; from generation to generation.

Then out of agape love, God mercifully made a second covenant, but this one was unconditional. It wasn't a covenant Adam could break. It was a covenant God the Father made with God the Son. And it would cover Adam's sins and all of mankind's. It was the Blood Covenant of Redemption.

The Covenant of Redemption aka the Adamic Covenant

In Genesis 3:15 God said to the serpent who tempted Eve, "*I will put enmity between you and the woman, between your seed and her seed; He shall bruise your head, and you shall bruise His heel."* As revealed in the Bible, the woman was the Virgin Mary and the promised seed of the woman, Jesus.

The Apostle Paul tells us in Romans 5:12, *"Therefore, just as sin entered the world through one man (Adam), and death through sin, and in this way death came to all people, because all have sinned."* And in 1 Corinthians 15:21-22 Paul shared the rest of the story, *"For since death came through a man, the resurrection of the dead comes also through a man. For as in Adam all die, so in Christ all will be made alive."* And this gift of eternal life was accomplished through the Adamic, unbreakable, blood covenant as outlined in Genesis 3:15.

The Virgin Mary

Isaiah prophesied in Chapter 17:14, *"Therefore the Lord himself will give you a sign: The virgin will conceive, and give birth to a son, and will call his name Immanuel."* And in Luke 1:27 we read, *"To a virgin pledged to be married to a man named Joseph, a descendent of David. The virgin's name was Mary."* Both passages place emphasis on the fact that Immanuel's mother was a virgin. In addition she is identified a virgin in the Islamic bible, the Qur'an. The Qur'an testifies to her immaculate conception and the virgin birth of Jesus.

With such prominence given to Mary's virginity, what was its significance? In Israel, an engaged virgin was considered the same thing as being married. If it became known during her engagement that she had premarital sex with another man, both she and the man would be stoned as adulterers. Sexual purity was of utmost importance. A sometime used ritual in the Hebrew culture sheds some light on this subject. Hebrew tradition reports parents keeping blood-stained sheets from a daughter's wedding night as proof of her virginity. Therefore, if ever accused of not being a virgin in order to obtain a divorce, the sheets could refute the claim.

Also, sometime in Middle Eastern history, the ancestors of Ishmael began examining engaged virgins. These exams became a sort of a premarital prerequisite. A virgin would be asked to lie down on a white sheet spread out before her. An impartial woman would be employed to inspect her hymen. If intact, it would be pierced and its blood poured out on the sheet. The stained sheet would be proof positive that the engaged girl was a virgin. The stained sheet ceremoniously would be taken outside of the room and waved before the groom's and the girl's families. If she wasn't a virgin, she could be stoned to death or have her throat cut. Her death would remove the family's shame of her being sexually impure.

Fast forward, as recorded in the book of Matthew, Mary was engaged when an angel informed her that she was pregnant. This news was frightening. As noted, engaged girls, pregnant with another man's baby, could be stoned. But Joseph, not wanting to expose any infidelity, considered a quiet divorce. However, an angel appeared to Joseph, too. The angel's appearance convinced Joseph of Mary's virginity and Immaculate Conception. Therefore, providentially, no further scrutiny was sought. Joseph's engagement with Mary remained secure.

The angel of the Lord told Joseph he wasn't to consummate their marriage until after the baby Jesus was born. But why? Maybe because the feet of the baby Jesus would break through Mary's virgin blood, ushering in the promised Covenant of Redemption. The Genesis statement relating to the bruising of His heel may well have referred in part to Jesus' birth, as well as Jesus' death, and ultimate resurrection..

The Virgin Birth and the Blood of Jesus

The Holy Spirit impregnated Mary and her Immaculate Conception confirmed Jesus as the Son of God. Mary's Immaculate Conception guaranteed that Jesus' blood was pure. Science has demonstrated that when a baby is conceived neither the sperm nor egg carry any blood. Blood creation begins when the egg and sperm unite in the fallopian tube. While in the placenta the fetus is protected from any flow of the mother's blood. The Bible is very clear that Jesus' DNA was produced by the Holy Spirit of God. Scientifically, it wasn't possible for any of Mary's stained blood to contaminate Jesus' blood. Jesus' blood was of divine origin and only his untainted blood could ever atone for man's sins.

God's conceived plan of redemption is identified in 1 Peter 1:19-29, *"But with the precious blood of Christ, a lamb without blemish or defect. He was chosen before the creation of the world, but was revealed in these last times for your sake."* As evident in this verse, and the verses in Genesis, in eternity past, God predestined His Son to become a human sacrifice. Adam and Eve's animal coverings shadowed in time, the Son of God's ultimate blood sacrifice on the altar of the cross.

As explained in Hebrews 9:22, *"Without the shedding of blood there is no forgiveness."* With the Jesus' death and resurrection, the sinful covenant unwittingly made with Satan by Adam was expunged. Jesus' atoning sacrifice removed mankind's sins all the way back to Adam. And all of the accuser's charges against God's elect were dropped. As the Psalmist wrote in Psalm 103:12, *"as far as the east is from the west, so far has he removed our transgressions from us."* And even more than this, Jesus' blood has forgiven all future sins.

"The one who enters by the gate."

An interesting passage of scripture is found in John chapter ten where Jesus is found conversing with some Pharisees. Jesus told them that anyone who doesn't enter the sheep pen by the gate, but climbs in by some other way, is a thief and robber. *"The one who enters by the gate is the shepherd of the sheep...Very truly I tell you, I am the gate for the sheep."*

By comparison, Jesus was telling them that through His conception, sinless life, and ultimate sacrifice on the cross, He was truly the gate. Besides Jesus, there is no one worthy to atone for mankind's sins. Singularly, Jesus is the gateway to salvation.

CHAPTER 2

THE NOAHIC AND ABRAHAMIC COVENANTS

Cain and Abel

Adam knew Eve and she bore him a son named Cain. Later she bore another son named Abel. Abel was a keeper of sheep, and Cain, a tiller of the ground. The boys' parents taught them about God and what type of sacrifices were acceptable to Him. When it came time to pay homage to God, Cain brought an offering from the ground, while Abel killed a first-born out of his flock. God honored Abel's sacrifice but not Cain's. Cain knew what he was supposed to offer but decided to offer a grain offering instead.

As their parents, Adam and Eve taught both boys that only blood sacrifices were acceptable to God as offerings. But instead of seeking forgiveness of his sins through a blood sacrifice, Cain wanted the fruits of his own labor to satisfy God's requirement. God assured Cain that his works were fruitless, and only a blood sacrifice would be acceptable. Cain didn't like the answer he was getting from God and got mad. God warned Cain, *"Sin lies at*

the door. And its desire is for you, but you should rule over it."
In other words, Cain's anger was like a crouching tiger ready to pounce. Cain didn't heed God's wisdom. He allowed anger and jealousy to rule his heart and murdered his brother.

Abel's grave site would be a constant reminder to the family of sin's devastating influence. God in his mercy blessed Adam and Eve, though, with another son they named Seth.

The Noahic Covenant

Seth's descendants must have understood and accepted God's plan of redemption. Because many years later, a descendent of Seth's, a righteous man named Noah was said to have "walked with God." However, the other descendants of Adam and Eve had become wildly wicked, corrupting all of God's creation. Enough so, that God decided to bring about a catastrophic flood. Noah, though, was God's friend and God promised to save him and his entire family from the inescapable judgment.

God asked Noah to build an ark. God's plans called for a three story-like barge. It was to be 450 feet long, 75 feet wide, and 45 feet high. By comparison the playing area of a football field is 300' x 160'. By faith, Noah and his sons, Shem, Ham and Japheth, built the enormous ark on dry land. It probably took somewhere between 50 and 75 years to build. The criticism received from those watching them was probably great.

"If you have no opposition in the place you serve,
you're serving in the wrong place."

G. Campbell Morgan

When finished, enigmatically, pairs of birds and animals were captured by Noah and his sons, and brought into the ark. They were to be saved from the imminent flood. Notably, in the midst of this devastating judgment, God delivered Noah and his family from the flood.

After the waters subsided, Noah stepped out onto dry land. He was grateful for having been spared from judgment and offered up to God an animal sacrifice.

Then Noah built an altar to the Lord and, taking some of all the clean animals and clean birds, he sacrificed burnt offerings on it. The Lord smelled the pleasing aroma and said in his heart: "*Never again will I curse the ground because of humans, even though every inclination of the human heart is evil from childhood. And never again will I destroy all living creatures, as I have done. As long as the earth endures, seedtime and harvest, cold and heat, summer and winter, day and night will never cease.*" Genesis 8:20-22.

God accepted Noah's sacrifice and this covenant offering set an example for Noah's descendants to emulate. And as identified, God made an everlasting covenant with Noah. God promised never again to destroy the planet by flood. And at this time, God established on earth the cycle of seasons. And as a sign of His perpetual and unconditional covenant with Noah, set a rainbow in the clouds.

God blessed Noah and gave him instructions to be fruitful and multiply, and to fill the earth. Also, in Genesis Chapter 9, this prophetic blessing was bestowed on Noah's sons, Shem, Ham and Japheth. In a way, the ark was illustrative of Christ. While divine judgment came upon the earth, the ark became a refuge for God's people.

The Abrahamic Covenant

Further into the book of Genesis is a story about Abram. Abram was a distant descendent of Noah's son, Shem. He lived around 2100 BC and Abram's family roots were in Ur of the Chaldeans. Ur was a city located on the Euphrates River in southern Mesopotamia. Its ruins are located in southern Iraq near the country of Kuwait.

After Abram was married, his father, Terah, took Abram, and his wife Sarai, a nephew named Lot, and traveled 600 miles northwest of Ur to a place called Haran, a city whose ruins lie within present-day Turkey. While living in Haran, Abram prospered and became rich. When Abram was 75 years old, the Lord spoke to him. The dialogue was recorded in Genesis 12:1-3. *"Leave your native country, your relatives, and your father's family, and go to the land I will show you. I will make you into a great nation, and I will bless you, and make your name great, and you will be a blessing. And I will bless them you bless, and curse him that curses you; and in you will all families of the earth be blessed."*

Through this covenant conversation, Abram was promised that he would be the progenitor of a great nation. Abram trusted in God's word, gathered his clan, and caravanned 400 miles southwest to a place in Canaan called Shechem, a town approximately 30 miles north of Jerusalem. There the Lord appeared to him again and said, "*Unto your seed (descendants) will I give this land."* Genesis 12:7. Abram believed God and built an altar at Shechem to honor Him.

God's Covenant Promise of Land to Abram's Descendants

Later Abram and his clan journeyed from Shechem to a mountain place between Bethel on the west and Ai on the east. And because of a severe famine in the land, the clan traveled even further south into Egypt. After spending some time in Egypt, Abram journeyed back to the place where he first set up camp. There Abram called on the name of the Lord, and the Lord made another covenant promise as described in Genesis 13:14-17. "*Look around from where you are, to the north and south, to the east and west. All the land that you see I will give to you and your offspring forever. I will make your offspring like the dust of the earth, so that if anyone could count the dust, then your offspring could be counted. Go, walk through the length and breadth of the land, for I am giving it to you."*

The place where Abram moved his clan was near Hebron under the great trees of Mamre. The grove was located about 19 miles southwest of Jerusalem. They pitched their tents. Here, Abram built another altar unto the Lord. There the Lord appeared to Abram in a vision, saying, "*I am your shield, your exceedingly great reward.*" And the Lord promised Abram a son from his own body. Then Abram was taken outside and instructed to look up toward heaven and count the number of stars. "*So shall your descendants be,*" said the Lord. Abram believed and God accounted it to him for righteousness.

Cutting Covenant

To validate these covenant promises, Abram was told to bring God a three year-old heifer, a three year-old female goat, a three year-old ram, a turtle dove and a young pigeon. The animals were to be killed and split down the middle. The haves were to be placed on the ground, positioned opposite of each other. The slaughtered turtle dove and pigeon were to be left whole. Abram did as God instructed. While the sacrifices were lying on the ground vultures came and Abram drove them away. What was God doing? God was preparing Abram for a covenant cutting ceremony. It was a cultural ritual and something which Abram was probably familiar. The prophet Jeremiah gives reference to this practice in Jeremiah 34:18-19.

The Lord revealed to Jeremiah that those who have violated my covenant, and have not fulfilled the terms of the covenant made before me, I will treat like the calf they cut in two and then walked between its pieces. Then the violators were identified as the leaders of Judah and Jerusalem, the court officials, the priests and all the people of the land who walked between the pieces of the calf. As with Abram, in this custom two parties laid out parts of a blood sacrifice on the ground and walked between them. This action was symbolic of each party agreeing to fulfill his covenant promise, and further agreeing to have the blood poured out of their life should they fail to honor their part.

As the sun set, God placed Abram into a deep sleep. He wasn't to be a participant in this sacred ceremony. While sleeping, God shared with Abram a strange, two-part dream. First, God's people were to be held in bondage for 400 years and then delivered with great wealth. Secondly, Abram saw something passing through the path of animal halves which he had killed and positioned on the ground. Whoever it was, it was walking alone through the sacrificed halves. As identified earlier, in covenant-making the passing through of sacrificed halves was symbolic of dying to oneself on behalf of the other person. Abram described the entity's brilliant glow as a smoking furnace and an intensely bright torch. What Abram actually witnessed was the pre-incarnate, eternal Son of God, clothed in all righteousness. Abram wasn't required to do anything. And his sleeping through the ritual, magnified the fact that God was making this unbreakable covenant with Himself. Normally two parties would pass between the sacrificed halves. But not during this ceremony. The pre-existing Son of God was the only one worthy enough to stand in for both God and Abram. And in this solitary act, God bound Himself to the covenant promises made to Abram. Afterwards, regardless of what Abram does or doesn't do in the future, God's promises remained unwavering.

Abram's Life Continued: Hagar and Ishmael

Fast forward, after trying for ten years to get pregnant, Abram's wife Sarai decided to give Abram (in marriage) an Egyptian slave named Hagar. Abram accepted, and took Hagar as a second wife to cherish, love and honor. Hagar became pregnant and Sarai became jealous. Sarai's jealousy caused her to mistreat Hagar. To protect herself and the baby, Hagar decided to run away. But an angel of the Lord appeared to Hagar and told her to go back and submit to Sarai. In return, she was told that her descendants would be too numerous to count. Hagar returned and delivered a baby boy named Ishmael. At the time of Ishmael's birth his father Abram was 86 years old.

God's Promise to Give Abram's Descendants the Land of Canaan

When Abram was 99 years old, the Lord appeared yet again to him and said, "*I am God Almighty; walk before me faithfully and be blameless. Then I will make my covenant between me and you and will greatly increase your numbers.*" Abram fell facedown before his Lord. Then God further clarified His covenant promises to Abram as recorded in Genesis 17:1-8.

"*As for me, this is my covenant with you: You will be the*

father of many nations. No longer will you be called Abram your name will be Abraham, for I have made you a father of many nations. I will make you very fruitful; I will make nations of you, and kings will come from you. I will establish my covenant as an everlasting covenant between me and you and your descendants after you for the generations to come, to be your God and the God of your descendants after you. The whole land of Canaan, where you now reside as a foreigner, I will give as an everlasting possession to you and your descendants after you; and I will be their God."

In this passage God gave Abram a covenant name. God added the *AH* in Abr*AH*am's name. In the Hebrew language the *AH* is a breathy sound, representing the very breath of God. Abraham's wife's name was changed from Sarai (meaning princess) to Sar*AH* meaning "princess of God."

That same year, the Lord visited Abraham again, making additional covenant promises. This time in a vision. God told Abraham that he would become the father of many nations, and that kings would come from his seed. Astoundingly, God promised to Abraham as an everlasting possession, all of the land in Canaan. God told Abraham, too, that his 99 year old wife, Sarah, would bear him a son. Abraham was skeptical. Regardless, God said she would bear him a son to be named Isaac and that the everlasting covenant made with Abraham would pass to Isaac, and then through his descendants. And as for Ishmael, he would become the father of twelve rulers and the progenitor of a great nation.

The Covenant Scar of Circumcision

As a sign of their covenant relationship, Abraham was told to cut covenant where the promise of his "seed" flowed. The scar from the circumcision would be a constant reminder of God's everlasting covenant with His chosen people. Abraham's future male descendants were all to be circumcised, confirming in their flesh, the acceptance of the covenant's blessing. To that end, all male babies were to be circumcised eight days from their birth. After hearing the additional promises of God, Abraham circumcised himself, his thirteen year old son, Ishmael, and every male in his household.

Covenant Scaring

Historically, covenant scaring identified a person as being more than one actually sees. In Dr. Richard Booker's book, *The Miracle of the Scarlet Thread*, covenant scars bore witness to a covenant's existence. In essence, the scar had a voice. It says, "There's more to me than meets the eye. If you're coming after me, you're also going to have to fight my covenant partner. And you don't know how big he is; so what are you going to do?" According to Richard Booker, African explorer Henry Stanley cut covenant 50 times with various chieftains. Every time he came across a hostile tribe, Henry raised his right arm. The fear of retribution from one of his covenant partners often persuaded hostile tribal leaders to reconsider their intent.

Jesus' Scars

In John 20:24-29 Jesus showed his physical scars to Thomas. *"Now Thomas, one of the Twelve, was not with the disciples when Jesus came. So the other disciples told him, 'We have seen the Lord!' But he said to them, 'Unless I see the nail marks in his hands and put my finger where the nails were, and put my hand into his side, I will not believe.' A week later his disciples were in the house again, and Thomas was with them. Though the doors were locked, Jesus came and stood among them and said, "Peace be with you!" Then he said to Thomas, "Put your finger here; see my hands. Reach out your hand and put it into my side. Stop doubting and believe." Thomas said to him, "My Lord and my God!" Then Jesus told him, "Because you have seen me, you have believed; blessed are those who have not seen and yet have believed."*

Jesus' scars bore testimony to the unbreakable blood covenant between the Father and Son which absolved sin.

The Three Visitors

Returning to our narrative about Abraham, weeks later the Lord appeared again to him. Genesis Chapter 18 records the events of this encounter. *While Abraham was camped by the shade trees in Mamre. It was during the heat of the day and Abraham was sitting just inside his tent's door. He lifted his eyes and saw three men approaching, appearing to stop by for a visit. Abraham ran to meet them, bowing himself to the ground and offering to bring them water to wash their feet. He then hurried into his tent and said to Sarah, "Quick, get three measures of the finest flour and knead it and bake some bread." Then he ran to the herd and selected a choice, tender calf, and gave it to a servant, who hurried to prepare it. He then brought some curds, and milk, and the calf that had been prepared, and set them before the three men."* Then the four of them sat down to enjoy a meal together. Sometime during the encounter the pre-incarnate Jesus revealed Himself to Abraham. As Lord, he asked Abraham where his wife was, and Abraham said she was inside the tent. Then the Lord told Abraham he would return in a year and at that time Sarah, who was beyond child birthing age, would bear Abraham a son. Sarah overheard the promise and was skeptical. She laughed. But then she was asked, *"Is anything too hard for the Lord?"* A year later, the promise came to pass. Abraham and Sarah had a boy they named Isaac. And when he was eight days old they had him circumcised.

Abraham, Covenant Breaker

After Isaac was born, his half-brother Ishmael received less attention and he became annoyed. He began mocking Isaac and Sarah became furious. She told Abraham to get rid of Hagar and her son. Sarah's son, not Hagar's, was going to be the son of Abraham's inheritance. The situation troubled Abraham. But the Lord told Abraham to let Hagar and her son go. His son Isaac would become the progenitor of the promises made to Abraham. And that his son Ishmael would become the progenitor of a great nation, too. So Abraham broke his marital covenant with Hagar, sending her and the boy away. As promised, God remained with

Hagar and her son. Hagar found an Egyptian wife for her son Ishmael. And as foretold by God, Ishmael became the father of twelve rulers and the progenitor of the Ishmaelites.

To the Ishmaelites, father Abraham was a covenant breaker. Hagar was much more than a surrogate mother, Hagar was Abraham's wife. Abraham's dismissing of her and his son Ishmael was reprehensible. At this point in time, the bad blood between the Arabs and Israelites began.

The Sacrifice of Isaac

While Isaac was still a boy, God tested Abraham's covenant promise of loyalty. God asked Abraham to sacrifice his son of promise to Him on a mountain altar. In essence God was saying, "As a covenant partner are you willing to give me your heart?" Just the thought of sacrificing his son must have been agonizing. However, the covenant he had with God required him to give up whatever was most dear to him. Taking his son's life was a tremendous sacrifice, even far greater than taking his own. But Abraham understood his covenant obligations, and though painfully difficult, he was obedient.

Abraham packed a donkey and took Isaac to the place God had ordained for the sacrifice. The place was on Mount Moriah.[1]

When they came close to the site, Abraham collected a knife

and possibly a pot with some live charcoal. It is easy to assume that he took the wood for the burnt offering and lifted it off the donkey's back, placing it on Isaac's shoulders. Like Christ, carrying His wooden cross up the hill to Calvary, Isaac carried the wood on his back. Together they climbed up the mountain to the altar of sacrifice. As they began their trek, Isaac inquired about the absence of a sacrificial lamb. And his father said, *"My son, God will provide for Himself a lamb for a burnt offering."* (This faith statement put into motion God's revelation of the substitutionary sacrifice of his own son.) When they arrived Abraham bound Isaac with a rope, laying his body on the fire wood. With Isaac resting on top of the altar, Abraham stretched out his arm to cut Isaac's throat. And just at the critical moment of taking his life, an angel of the Lord stopped him. Abraham had proven his faithfulness.

Isaac, a Type of Christ

In this account, Isaac foreshadowed the role of Christ. He could have resisted and wrestled away from his father, but Isaac was obedient, even if it meant his own death. After the angelic halt, Abraham looked up and saw a ram caught by its horns in the thicket. He untied Isaac and no doubt hugged him. Abraham slew the ram, and like Jesus, the ram became a substitutionary sacrifice. The shed blood of the substitute ram sealed the everlasting Abrahamic Covenant.

---

[1] Mt. Moriah is located in Old City Jerusalem. Sitting atop of the hill today is the Temple Mount, a place where the Jewish temple once stood. The same area today can be reached through eleven gates, one for non-Muslims, and the rest for Muslims. Israeli police guard the entrances.

The Cornerstone of Scripture

In Hebrews 6:13-14 we read, "*For when God made a promise to Abraham, because He could swear by no one greater, He swore by Himself, saying, 'Surely blessing I will bless you, and multiplying I will multiply you.'* " Then the Lord made this profound statement to Abraham in Genesis 22:18, "*In your seed all the nations will be blessed because you obeyed my voice.*"

This Abrahamic promise is the cornerstone connecting all of biblical history and is its principal focus. In fact, every sacrificial act, every Hebrew feast, and many of the recorded lives in the Old Testament, foreshadowed this blessed promise. Because with the advent of Jesus, through Abraham's "seed," all nations were blessed. As reiterated by the Apostle Paul in Galatians 3:16, "*Now to Abraham and his seed were the promises made. He does not say, 'And to seeds,' as of many, but as of one, 'And to your Seed,' who is Christ.*" And as chronicled in the Gospel of Luke, Jesus's mothers' genealogy (seed) was traced all the way back to the progenitor, Abraham.

The Abrahamic Covenant

In review, these are the main covenant promises God made with Abraham.

- God called Abraham from Haran to a land that He would give him. The territorial dimensions of that land are stated in Genesis 15:18.

- God made an unconditional promise of innumerable descendants who would become great nations and kings. And this promise was made to Abraham when he was 75 and childless.

- God promised to bless Abraham and all the families of the earth through his seed. A promise fulfilled in Jesus' advent, death and resurrection.

CHAPTER 3

ISAAC AND JACOB, CONVEYORS OF THE ABRAHAMIC COVENANT

Abraham's Son, Isaac

After Isaac became a man, Abraham didn't want Isaac to marry a pagan-worshipping Canaanite women. So he had a faithful servant and an accompanying party travel back to Haran to find a bride for Isaac. They traveled by caravan for days before stopping to rest their camels by a well near the city of Nahor. At the well, Abraham's servant engaged in conversation with a beautiful young woman, a virgin whose name was Rebeckah. During their conversation he learned she was related to Abraham's brother, Nahor (the city's namesake). After talking with her, Abraham's servant gave Rebeckah an expensive gold nose ring and two solid gold bracelets. She then led the servant and his caravan back to her home where she introduced them to her brother, Laban.

The servant told Laban about Abraham's wealth and his wishes for his son, Isaac. After listening, Laban and his father,

Bethuel, agreed that Rebeckah should become Isaac's bride. The servant was so grateful to God for allowing him to accomplish his mission that he bowed his head to the ground and gave homage to his Lord. Before departing, the servant gave Rebeckah gifts of clothing, and silver and gold jewelry. Also, he gave more precious things to her mother and brother.

Rebeckah became Isaac's wife and he loved her. At the time of their marital union, Isaac was 40 years old. Rebeckah wasn't able to conceive, so Isaac pleaded with God to allow her to get pregnant. God heard his prayers and opened her womb. She gave birth to twin boys, Esau and Jacob. Esau was born first.

While the twins were growing up, a famine came upon the land and Isaac contemplated moving his clan to Egypt. We find in Genesis 26:3-6 that the Lord appeared to Isaac and said, "*Do not go down to Egypt; live in the land where I tell you to live. Stay in this land for a while, and I will be with you and will bless you. For to you and your descendants I will give all these lands and will confirm the oath I swore to your father Abraham. I will make your descendants as numerous as the stars in the sky and will give them all these lands, and through your offspring all nations on earth will be blessed, because Abraham obeyed me and did everything I required of him, keeping my commands, my decrees and my instructions.*" So Isaac stayed where they were in Gerar.

Appearing to Isaac at night, the Lord confirmed His covenant promise found in Genesis 26:24-25 saying, "*I am the God of your father Abraham. Do not be afraid, for I am with you; I will bless you and will increase the number of your descendants for the sake of my servant Abraham.*" In the morning Isaac built an altar unto the Lord and worshipped Him. Isaac had tents pitched at that location and asked his servants to dig (and possibly re-open) wells previously dug by the servants of Abraham. The place was called Beersheba, located about 75 miles southwest of Jerusalem.

While the twins were still at home, Jacob persuaded Esau to trade Esau's birthright for some bread and stew made out of lentils. At the time Esau didn't consider his birthright to be important. But it was very significant. The birthright transferred to the firstborn son all of the father's authority and responsibilities. In addition, the firstborn inherited twice as much as that of the other sons. So it was a big deal.

Isaac's Blessing upon Jacob (Genesis 27:28-29)

After Isaac had grown old and became blind, his wife Rebeckah, and their son Jacob, connived a prophetic blessing from Isaac which was intended for Esau. Isaac was deceived. Believing he was blessing Esau, he was tricked into blessing Jacob. Blind Isaac said to his son Jacob, "*May God give you heaven's dew and earth's richness - an abundance of grain and new wine. May nations serve you and peoples bow down to you. Be lord over your brothers, and may the sons of your mother bow down to you. May those who curse you be cursed and those who bless you be blessed.*"

The manipulation initiated by Rebeckah (Esau's mother), produced a damaging and dangerous wedge between the twins. Esau held a grudge and in fact, Esau sought to kill Jacob. In order to put some distance between the boys, Rebeckah decided to send Jacob away to Padan Aram. There Jacob was to connect with her brother Laban and find for himself a bride. Simultaneously, Esau went to Ishmael's clan and married one of his Canaanite daughters.

Jacob's Ladder

Along his way to Padan Aram, Jacob stopped to rest and fell asleep. He dreamt that a ladder was anchored on earth with its top reaching to heaven. On the ladder, angels were ascending and descending. The Lord revealed Himself to Jacob and said, *"I am the Lord, the God of your father Abraham and the God of Isaac. I will give you and your descendants the land on which you are lying. Your descendants will be like the dust of the earth, and you will spread out to the west and to the east, to the north and to the south. All peoples on earth will be blessed through you and your offspring. I am with you and will watch over you wherever you go, and I will bring you back to this land. I will not leave you until I have done what I have promised you."* God's confirmation of the Abrahamic Covenant to Jacob was pretty amazing since Jacob was a bit of a scoundrel. But scoundrel or not, Jacob came under the unbreakable, unshakable, covenant God made with his grandfather. The same three blessings promised to Abraham and Isaac were reiterated to Jacob; 1) land, 2) proliferation of descendants, and 3) ultimate blessing.

When Jacob awoke from his sleep, he anointed with oil the stone he was using as a pillow. He was in awe of God's presence and felt that he had been resting on the actual gate to heaven. He named the place Bethel, which was about six miles north of Jerusalem. And in return for God's covenant promises, Jacob promised to give God one-tenth of all that God provided him.

Jacob and Rachel

Arriving at his destination, Jacob encountered a Hebrew shepherdess named Rachel. He fell in love with her and desired her hand in marriage. But before marrying her, Jacob was asked as a dowry to serve Rachel's father (Laban) for seven years. So he agreed. Leah's father then tricked Jacob. He made Jacob marry Rachel's oldest sister first whose name was Leah. After they had consummated their marriage, Laban gave Rachel to Jacob with this caveat; seven more years of service.

Leah bore Jacob four sons, Reuben, Simeon, Levi and Judah. Reuben was the oldest. Rachel wasn't able to conceive and became jealous of Leah. So she gave her handmaiden Bilhah to her husband as a concubine and Jacob and Bilhah had two sons, Dan and Naphtali. Leah then became jealous of Rachel's maneuver and gave her handmaiden, Zilpah, to Jacob as another concubine. Jacob slept with Zilpah and she gave birth to sons, Gad and Asher. Jacob and Leah had two more children; a son named Zebulun and a daughter named Dinah. Finally, God allowed Rachel to get pregnant. She conceived and bore a son whom they named

Joseph. Jacob favored Joseph and Joseph's half-brothers became jealous of him.

After leaving Laban God continued to bless Jacob and he became a very wealthy man. But money couldn't clear his conscience. Cheating Esau troubled his soul and Jacob desired forgiveness. A meeting was arranged to meet up with his twin brother. Justifiably, Jacob was apprehensive about facing Esau. In an attempt to clear his conscience, Jacob sent servants out ahead with a huge herd of domestic animals while Jacob and his family stayed cautiously behind.

Jacob's New Covenant Name

The night before meeting up with his brother, Jacob was alone and the Lord wrestled with him in a dream. When daybreak came Jacob wouldn't let go of the Lord. So the Lord touched Jacob's hip socket and it went out of joint. Then the Lord said, *"Let me go, for the day breaks."* But Jacob said, *"I will not let You go unless You bless me!"* Then the Lord told him that his name would no longer be Jacob, but Israel. Then Jacob asked for the Lord's name and was told, *"Why is it that you ask about My name?"* And then He blessed him right there. Jacob named the place Peniel meaning, *"I have seen God face to face, and my life is preserved."*

Jacob's Reunion with Esau

The next day the two brothers met. Unbeknownst to Jacob, his brother was equally successful and rich. Esau arrived with

400 men and Jacob sheepishly bowed before him. Esau embraced Jacob and as they talked Esau dismissed Jacob's extravagant gift of livestock. He told his brother thanks, but it wasn't necessary. Still, Jacob insisted and eventually Esau acquiesced. It is assumed that the brothers buried the hatchet. Regardless, contempt remained between Esau's descendants and Jacob's because Jacob stole their progenitor's birthright. Esau's descendants make up the majority of Arab nations living in the Middle East today.

Abrahamic Covenant Transferred to Jacob

Sometime later, God directed Israel (Jacob) to leave Shechem and journey back to Bethel. There he was to purify his household and build an altar unto God. Through this act of worship, Jacob fulfilled his vow. God appeared to Jacob again reiterating what He had told him earlier. We read about the dialogue in Genesis 35:9-15. *"After Jacob returned from Padan Aram, God appeared to him again and blessed him. God said to him, 'Your name is Jacob, but you will no longer be called Jacob; your name will be Israel.' " So he named him Israel. And God said to him, "I am God Almighty; be fruitful and increase in number. A nation and a community of nations will come from you, and kings will be among your descendants. The land I gave to Abraham and Isaac I also give to you, and I will give this land to your descendants after you." Then God went up from him at the place where he had talked with him. Jacob set up a stone pillar at the place where God had talked with him, and he poured out a drink offering on it; he also poured oil on it. Jacob called the place where God had talked with him Bethel."*

Israel's Son, Joseph

Later Israel's clan left Bethel for Bethlehem and as they journeyed, Rachel was with child. She was late in her pregnancy and along the way went into hard labor. While giving birth to Jacob's twelfth son, Benjamin, she died. Jacob set a pillar on her grave.

Rachel's other son, Joseph, was a dreamer. Early in life Joseph had a dream where he ruled over his parents and brothers. After hearing the dream, his brothers became angry, taking offense to the authoritative interpretation. Joseph was favored by his father who made him a coat of many colors. This fueled the brothers' scorn for him even more. The coat given to Joseph had significance. It was symbolic of rights normally bestowed on a first born son, making Reuben subordinate to his half-brother.

Twenty Pieces of Silver

Joseph and his brothers were sheep and goat herders. One day Israel asked Joseph to check on his brothers who were out in a distant field. Joseph journeyed to find them, and when he did, his brothers accused him of spying on them. The brothers stripped him of his coat and tossed Joseph down a dry well. No doubt Joseph was scared. Some of his brothers wanted to kill him but Reuben wouldn't allow it. When Reuben was out of sight, Judah convinced the others to sell Joseph as a slave to some Ishmaelite traders. When the merchants stopped, Joseph was traded for 20 pieces of silver. The brothers then dipped his exquisite coat in animal's blood to show their father when they returned home.

They told Israel that they stumbled upon the bloody coat and surmised that Joseph had been attacked and killed by a wild animal. It was an incredibly cruel thing they did to Joseph, and equally unkind, the lie they told to their father. The brothers would have to live with their guilty consciences.

Unbeknownst to his brothers, Joseph found favor as a slave with an Egyptian master. He was placed in a position of authority over his master's house. On several occasions his master's wife tried to seduce Joseph, but each time Joseph rejected her advances. However, one time she grabbed at his coat and as he fled, it came off his shoulders. Out of revenge for Joseph not accepting her advances to have sex, she accused him of attempted rape. She showed her husband Joseph's outer coat as proof of his presence. Joseph's master had little choice but to take his wife's word and had Joseph incarcerated.[1]

While in jail God's watchful eye remained evident on Joseph. Joseph became the chief jailer's helper. While serving in that capacity two of Pharaoh's servants became imprisoned.

Each had a dream and they asked Joseph to interpret them. Joseph prayed to God for an interpretation. God revealed that one of them would live (the chief butler) but the other would die (the chief baker). Joseph revealed God's interpretation to them and both happened as foretold.

---

[1] Like Joseph, Christians need to feel secure even when facing persecutions and challenges. Although the suffering is real and painful, beyond the circumstances is a strong and devoted God. Despite all of the betrayal in his life Joseph trusted God for protection and remained rooted in his faith.

Sometime later, the Pharaoh of Egypt had a troubling dream. It involved seven fat cows and seven of the straggliest looking lean cows, one could ever image. The lean cows devoured the fat cows but remained as thin and ugly as ever. Pharaoh sought an interpretation, but none of his counsel was wise enough to interpret the dream. Then the Pharaoh's chief butler remembered Joseph. He told Pharaoh about Joseph and his uncanny ability to interpret dreams. The ruler summoned Joseph, who came and listened to Pharaoh tell his dream. Then Joseph prayed to God for an interpretation. God revealed to Joseph that there would be seven incredible years for growing crops, followed by seven years of devastating drought. The drought would devour everything grown the seven previous years. Joseph shared God's interpretation and the Pharaoh believed Joseph. A plan was needed and Pharaoh gave Joseph the task of planning and executing a strategy.

Pharaoh said to Joseph, "*Since God has made all this known to you, there is no one so discerning and wise as you. You shall be in charge of my palace, and all my people are to submit to your orders. Only with respect to the throne will I be greater than you. I hereby put you in charge of the whole land of Egypt." Then Pharaoh took his signet ring from his finger and put it on Joseph's finger. He dressed him in robes of fine linen and put a gold chain around his neck. He had him ride in a chariot as his second-in-command,] and people shouted before him, "Make way!" Thus he put him in charge of the whole land of Egypt. Then Pharaoh said to Joseph, "I am Pharaoh, but without your word no one will lift hand or foot in all Egypt." Pharaoh gave Joseph the daughter of a priest to be his wife. And Joseph went throughout the land of Egypt.* (Genesis 41:39-45) So in one day's time, Joseph went from being a prisoner in jail, to becoming the second in command over all of Egypt.

Divine Interruption

By orchestrating Joseph to become an Egyptian ruler, God preserved Israel's clan and Abraham's inheritance. During the predicted famine, Joseph's family was in Canaan where they ran out of food. The clan found themselves needing to purchase grain which was stored in Egypt. So Israel sent ten of Joseph's bothers into Egypt to buy grain.

When they arrived the brothers encountered Joseph but they did not recognize him. He was older now and dressed in Egyptian garb as a decision-making ruler. Joseph recognized them and his heart was moved. However, instead of identifying himself, he decided to communicate through a Hebrew interpreter. Curious to know if his brothers were still as mean as they once were, Joseph tested them. As a ruse, he had them jailed as spies. After questioning, Joseph discovered that his youngest brother, Benjamin, and his father were still alive. Knowing this, Joseph allowed them to purchase the grain they needed and return home. But with a caveat. Joseph kept his brother Simeon as a ransom until they returned with Benjamin.

Back home they had to convince their father to let Benjamin return to Egypt. The brothers then left their home and returned with their younger brother. When Joseph saw Benjamin his heart was stirred. He wanted to reveal himself but decided to put his brothers through one more test.

Joseph ordered their donkeys be loaded with bags of grain as well as the money brought to purchase the grain. In essence, the grain became a gift. But unbeknownst to the brothers, Joseph secretly had his chalice placed in Benjamin's sack of grain. When they started journeying home, Joseph's soldiers stopped them, accusing one of them for stealing the chalice. The soldiers said, *"Why have you repaid evil for good?"* The brothers were aghast and replied, *"with whomever of your servants it is found, let him die, and the rest of us slaves."* So Joseph's men ushered them back for an inspection. As each man opened his sack the chalice fell out of Benjamin's sack.

Repentance

Judah, the brother who suggested trading Joseph for 20 pieces of silver, came to his little brother's rescue. Judah confessed to Joseph the brother's darkest sin of deception and pleaded for Benjamin's life. Joseph listened to Judah's repentant heart and was greatly moved. At that point, Joseph ordered everyone out of the room except his brothers. He couldn't stand the charade any longer and wanted to speak with them privately. While weeping out loud, he revealed himself to them, asking fervently, *"Does my father still live?"* But they were too afraid to answer.
Divine Providence (Genesis 45:5-15)

Joseph said to them, "*And now, do not be distressed and do not be angry with yourselves for selling me here, because it was to save lives that God sent me ahead of you. For two years now there has been famine in the land, and for the next five years there will be no plowing and reaping. But God sent me ahead of you to preserve for you a remnant on earth and to save your lives by a great deliverance. So then, it was not you who sent me here, but God. He made me a father to Pharaoh, lord of his entire household and ruler of all Egypt. Now hurry back to my father and say to him, 'This is what your son Joseph says: God has made me lord of all Egypt. Come down to me; don't delay. You shall live in the region of Goshen and be near me—you, your children and grandchildren, your flocks and herds, and all you have. I will provide for you there, because five years of famine are still to come. Otherwise you and your household and all who belong to you will become destitute. You can see for yourselves, and so can my brother Benjamin, that it is really I who am speaking to you. Tell my father about all the honor accorded me in Egypt and about everything you have seen. And bring my father down here quickly.' Then he threw his arms around his brother Benjamin and wept, and Benjamin embraced him, weeping. And he kissed all his brothers and wept over them. Afterward his brothers talked with him.*"

Joseph interceded for his family, asking Pharaoh if his father's clan could live on the land in Goshen. Pharaoh approved and Israel's clan moved to Egypt. By Joseph's divine interruptions, the covenant seed of Abraham was preserved.

Comparison of Joseph and Jesus

In the Old Testament many individuals typified something about the future Messiah. These are a few of the ways Joseph and Jesus' lives paralleled each other.

- Both Joseph and Jesus were first born sons prophesied to become rulers.

- Both were falsely accused.

- Joseph's brother Reuben wanted to rescue him and Pilate wanted to rescue Jesus.

- Joseph was sold as a slave to an Egyptian for 20 pieces of silver, the price of a slave, and Jesus was betrayed for 30 pieces of silver.

- While in jail, Joseph predicted that one man would live and the other die. On the cross, Jesus predicted that one of the men being executed with him would have eternal life, the other would not.

- The King of Egypt exalted Joseph to rule over the land and Jesus was exalted by the Father to bring all people under His rule.

- Joseph's brothers did not recognize him, and Jesus' own people didn't recognize him.

- The malicious intent Joseph's brothers had for him, God meant for good. The same is true of the evil Jesus' own people intended for him. God used Jesus' sacrifice to overcome their sin and spiritual death.

- Joseph's peculiar circumstances saved his family and the nation of Israel. And Jesus' unfathomable sacrifice on the cross saved mankind from being eternally separated from God.

CHAPTER 4

MOSES' CALLING

Disobedience and Enslavement

Over time, Joseph's generation passed away and the Israelites living in the land of Goshen lost sight of God. They began worshipping pagan gods and their rejection of the Lord resulted in enslavement. However, around 1250 B.C. God mercifully resumed the covenant made with Abraham. In keeping His promise of advancing Abraham's seed, God called Moses to lead the Israelites out of their bondage in Egypt.

Moses was born a Hebrew but raised by Pharaoh's daughter as an Egyptian. When fully grown, Moses was drawn back to his Hebrew roots. He killed an Egyptian taskmaster for being too brutal with a Hebrew slave. His traitorous act banned Moses from Pharaoh's family, and in fact, Pharaoh sought to kill Moses. Knowing he was a wanted man, Moses fled to the land of Midian. The Midianites were descendants of Abraham and his second wife, Keturah.

Moses arrived in Midian and sat down by a well. There he encountered seven daughters who had come to draw water. All of them were daughters of the priest of Midian. While attempting to draw water, their efforts were thwarted by shepherds attempting to drive them away. But Moses stood up for them and the shepherds backed off. Moses then drew water for them and their flocks. After returning home, the daughters told their father about the Egyptian who helped them. Jethro, their father, invited Moses to stay with the clan and soon offered his daughter Zipporah to be Moses' bride. Moses married her and stayed in Midian for 40 years. While living there, the Pharaoh who sought to kill Moses died.

Bondage in Egypt

Back in Egypt, the Israelites continued serving as slaves for the Egyptians. The Bible stated that they were in grievous bondage. So the Israelites cried out to God. Their repentant cries and pleas for relief reached God, rejuvenating the everlasting covenant God had made with Abraham, Isaac, and Jacob.

The Burning Bush

While Moses was tending to Jethro's flock in Horeb, his eyes were drawn to a most unusual sight. A flame of fire was burning inside a bush, except the bush wasn't burning. Out of curiosity, Moses drew near to this supernatural phenomenon. But he was stopped in his tracks! In Exodus, Chapter 3, from inside the bush,

God said emphatically, "*Moses, Moses, stay back, take off your sandals because where you are standing is holy ground. I am the God of your father, the God of Abraham, the God of Isaac and the God of Jacob.*" At this, Moses hid his face, because he was afraid to look at God. "*I have indeed seen the misery of my people in Egypt. I have heard them crying out because of their slave drivers, and I am concerned about their suffering. So I have come down to rescue them from the hand of the Egyptians and to bring them up out of that land into a good and spacious land, a land flowing with milk and honey—the home of the Canaanites, Hittites, Amorites, Perizzites, Hivites and Jebusites. And now the cry of the Israelites has reached me, and I have seen the way the Egyptians are oppressing them. So now, go. I am sending you to Pharaoh to bring my people the Israelites out of Egypt.*"

Moses replied, "*Who am I that I should go to Pharaoh and bring the Israelites out of Egypt?*" **And God said,** "*I will be with you. And this will be the sign to you that it is I who have sent you: When you have brought the people out of Egypt, you will worship God on this mountain.*" Moses said to God, "*Suppose I go to the Israelites and say to them, 'The God of your fathers has sent me to you,' and they ask me, 'What is his name?' Then what shall I tell them?*" God said to Moses, *'I Am Who I Am.' This is what you are to say to the Israelites: 'I Am has sent me to you.'* God also said to Moses, "*Say to the Israelites, 'The Lord, the God of your fathers—the God of Abraham, the God of Isaac and the God of Jacob—has sent me to you.' This is my name forever, the name you shall call me from generation to generation.*"

"Go, assemble the elders of Israel and say to them, 'The Lord, the God of your fathers—the God of Abraham, Isaac and Jacob—appeared to me and said: I have watched over you and have seen what has been done to you in Egypt. And I have promised to bring you up out of your misery in Egypt into the land of the Canaanites, Hittites, Amorites, Perizzites, Hivites and Jebusites—a land flowing with milk and honey.' The elders of Israel will listen to you. Then you and the elders are to go to the king of Egypt and say to him, 'The Lord, the God of the Hebrews, has met with us. Let us take a three-day journey into the wilderness to offer sacrifices to the Lord our God.' But I know that the king of Egypt will not let you go unless a mighty hand compels him. So I will stretch out my hand and strike the Egyptians with all the wonders that I will perform among them. After that, he will let you go. "And I will make the Egyptians favorably disposed toward this people, so that when you leave you will not go empty-handed. Every woman is to ask her neighbor and any woman living in her house for articles of silver and gold and for clothing, which you will put on your sons and daughters. And so you will plunder the Egyptians."

As God predicted, through a series of ten devastating and relentless plagues, all aimed at repudiating ten distinct Egyptian gods, Pharoah finally let God's people go. The final plague was the death of Egypt's first born and all of its first born animals. With that plague, Egypt's Pharaoh finally allowed Moses, the nomadic multitude of enslaved Israelites, and their entire herds of livestock, to leave the land of Goshen.[1]

The Night of Passover

On the night of God's final judgment against Egypt's Pharaoh, all of the Hebrew households were told to take a first born male lamb or goat without blemish, and kill it in the evening. Some of the animal's blood was to be applied to their home's two side posts (vertically) and the upper door post (horizontally). Then, as directed, an entire lamb, its head, legs, and internal organs, was to be roasted by fire. Once roasted the families were to eat the lamb's flesh with unleavened bread and bitter herbs. And if any of the lamb remained until morning, it was to be burned. Anticipating the order to leave Egypt, all family members were required to be fully dressed. By faith, the families did as Moses instructed. The applied blood prevented death's access to those inside their homes. As predicted, the angel of death passed over the Hebrew households but entered those of the pagan worshipping Egyptians. The twelfth chapter of Exodus explains the protective nature of the applied blood.

The Lord said to Moses and Aaron in Egypt, "This month is to be for you the first month, the first month of your year. Tell the whole community of Israel that on the tenth day of this month each man is to take a lamb for his family, one for each household.

---

[1] The book of Genesis ended with Jacob's family finding refuge in the land of Goshen. Goshen was located in the eastern delta of the Nile River, a very fertile area in north eastern Egypt. After Joseph's death, the rulers of Egypt forgot about him and began fearing the growing numbers of Israelites. To keep them under control, they enslaved them. Their bondage wasn't a complete surprise. During a vision to Abram back in Genesis 15:13, the four hundred years of slavery in Egypt had been foretold. Their bondage was judgment for being disobedient. But in Genesis 15:14, as part of Abrahamic Covenant, God told Abram that after the judgment period the people would come out of captivity with great wealth. However, to do required a deliverer.

If any household is too small for a whole lamb, they must share one with their nearest neighbor, having taken into account the number of people there are. You are to determine the amount of lamb needed in accordance with what each person will eat. The animals you choose must be year-old males without defect, and you may take them from the sheep or the goats. Take care of them until the fourteenth day of the month, when all the members of the community of Israel must slaughter them at twilight. Then they are to take some of the blood and put it on the sides and tops of the door frames of the houses where they eat the lambs... it is the Lord's Passover. "On that same night I will pass through Egypt and strike down every firstborn of both people and animals, and I will bring judgment on all the gods of Egypt. I am the Lord. The blood will be a sign for you on the houses where you are, and when I see the blood, I will pass over you. No destructive plague will touch you when I strike Egypt."

The death of Pharaoh's first born and all of Egypt's first born, finally brought Pharaoh to his knees. He finally agreed to let God's covenant people go. By applying the lamb's blood to their door posts, and eating the sacrificed lamb without blemish, the Israelites had renewed their covenant status with God. So through Moses, God made good on His covenant promise to Abraham.

Pharaoh's Change of Heart

As the exiting Israelites approached the Red Sea, Pharaoh changed his mind and sent chariot driven militia to bring them back. To thwart their approaching attack, God miraculously parted the waters of the Red Sea. In pursuit of the Israelites, Egyptian chariots and soldiers entered the parted sea. But as soon as the Israelites finished crossing ahead of them, the contained waves were unleashed, crashing down on the militia. And all of the enemy drowned. This miracle made God's name known among the heathen nations, and justifiably so, caused them to fear the Israelites.

The Exodus

This is a very abridged account. On their exodus journey to the land of promise, the Israelites had to pass through the Saini Desert. By appearing as a thick cloud during the day, God protected them from the intense heat. At night, with a fiery presence, God provided them with radiant heat. God fed them with manna and summoned quail for them to catch and eat. During their prolonged journey, Moses received the Ten Commandments, and under God's direction, instituted Jewish law.

When Moses first encountered the reluctant Pharaoh of Egypt, he was 80 years old. For another 40 years, operating under God's protection and presence, Moses led the Israelites across the Sinai Peninsula. When he died, Moses was 120.

CHAPTER 5

THE MOSAIC/SINAI COVENANT

The Mosaic or Sinai Covenant is a conditional covenant made between God and the nation of Israel. Moses was the covenant's intermediary. It was made on Mount Sinai and therefore referred to as the Sinai Covenant. At its inception, God reminded the people that His blessings were conditioned on their obedience and punishment would be their remuneration for disobedience. The people of Israel acknowledged both aspects of the covenant and told God they would obey.

The Mosaic covenant centered on God's promise to make Israel a kingdom of priests and a holy nation. As worshippers of the true God, they were to be a holy people, separated from the pagan world that existed all around them. To guide them, God gave Moses His laws, including the Ten Commandments. The commandments and laws revealed to the people their sinful nature, pointing them to the need of repentance. And to that end, God gave Moses a command to implement a sacrificial system that dealt, temporarily, with the penalty of sin.

God's Provisional Covenant

After a couple of months of wandering in the desert, Moses was summoned by God to meet Him on the top of a nearby mountain. Moses went up the mountain to pray and the Lord called out to him saying, "*This is what you are to say to the descendants of Jacob and what you are to tell the people of Israel: 'You yourselves have seen what I did to Egypt, and how I carried you on eagles' wings and brought you to myself. Now if you obey me fully and keep my covenant, then out of all nations you will be my treasured possession. Although the whole earth is mine, you will be for me a kingdom of priests and a holy nation.' These are the words you are to speak to the Israelites.*" So Moses descended from the mountain and summoned the elders of the people. He set before them all the words the Lord had commanded him to speak. And the people responded, "*We will do everything the Lord has said.*"

On the mountain God told Moses that he would appear to the people in a dense cloud, allowing the people to hear his voice. When Moses returned, he warned the people to take three days and consecrate themselves before the Lord appeared. They did, and on the third day, the people witnessed in a thick cloud, thunder and lightning; the mountain trembled and billowed with thick smoke. And there were sounds of celestial trumpets. Then God's voice spoke out the Ten Commandments. The people listened afar, trembling in fear. Then God continued a private conversation concerning his laws with Moses. The Lord shared with Moses that on his journey an angel would go before him, showing

Moses the way. And that if Moses listened carefully and obeyed the angel's commands, God would be an enemy to Moses' enemies, opposing any entity that faced Moses. God promised to send His terror out ahead of Moses, and throw into confusion every resisting nation Moses encountered. And if the people worshipped only God, His blessing would be on their provisions of food and water. There would be no sickness, miscarriages, or barrenness. And God shared with Moses that Israel's borders would extend from the Red Sea to the Mediterranean, and from the Negev to the River Euphrates.

Israel Affirms the Covenant

After speaking with the people, God told Moses to ascend the mountain with Aaron and two of his sons, and 70 elders to worship from afar. After Moses shared with the people the laws God had revealed to him, the people responded with one voice, *"Everything the Lord has said we will do."*

Moses then wrote down all the laws the Lord had told him. On the next morning, Moses got up early and built an altar at the foot of the mountain, setting up twelve stone pillars representing the twelve tribes of Israel. Moses offered up burnt offerings and sacrificed young bulls as fellowship offerings unto the Lord. He took half of the blood and put it in bowls, and the other half he splashed against the altar. Then Moses read the words and laws to the people and they responded, *"We will do everything the Lord has said; we will obey."* Moses then took some blood and sprinkled it on the written laws and on the people saying, *"This is the blood of the covenant that the Lord has made with you in accordance with all these words."* Did you notice? Something very different happened here. Moses sprinkled blood directly onto the people. With the direct application of blood the covenant became personal. As such, God told Moses, *"have them make a sanctuary for me, and I will dwell among them* (Exodus 25:8)." Incredibly, by covenant, the God of all Creation agreed to dwell among His people.

Then Moses and his protégé, Joshua, Aaron and the invited elders ascended part way up the mountain, and in the presence of holy God, shared a covenant meal. Then God said to Moses, *"Come up to me on the mountain and stay here, and I will give you the tablets of stone with the law and commandments I have written for their instruction."* While the others stayed behind, Moses went up the mountain with Joshua and the glory of God appeared to Moses in a cloud of consuming fire. After seven days on the mountain, Moses was summoned to very top. There he spent 40 days and nights in the presence of God.

On Mount Sinai, God instructed Moses how to make and equip an earthly sanctuary called a Tabernacle. Accompanying the building instructions were very specific requirements for the items to be placed near and inside the Tabernacle. Also, God gave Moses instructions for the creation of an earthly priesthood where Aaron was to be appointed by God as high priest. In addition, Moses was told how to conduct various types of required sacrifices. Once the Tabernacle was completed, and the earthly priesthood established,

Moses was told to sprinkle sacrificial blood over the Tabernacle, all of its furnishings, and the administering priests. The applied blood would confirm and seal their covenant.

When God finished speaking, Moses was given two tablets of law inscribed on their fronts and back by the finger of God. Sadly, while Moses was on the mountain with God, Aaron and the people commited a grievous sin against God. And God's righteous indignation was kindled greatly. Moses was instructed to go back down the mountain and witness the corruption.

The Golden Calf

While Moses was out of sight the people had an idol created to worship and to offer sacrifices. They encouraged Aaron to cast a calf from the gold they brought out of Egypt, and unbelievably, he did. When Moses and Joshua arrived back at the encampment the people were dancing wildly before the calf. Moses lost it! He threw the tablets to the ground and they shattered. He took the golden calf and burned it, grinding it into a powder. He sprinkled the powder into the water and made the people drink the bitter mixture. Then Moses instructed the Levites to "strap a sword" and kill those who rebelled against the Lord. That day about 3,000 people were slain. Moses then interceded for the rebellious Israelites, reminding God of His covenant promises. God agreed to spare the people but sent a plague among the people as punishment.

Moses then began the trek toward the land promised to the patriarchs. But before leaving Moses returned once more to Mount

Sinai. At the top of the mountain, Moses bowed and asked God to forgive the stiff-necked people. And on that day the Lord made this covenant with Moses.

Mosaic Covenant

The Lord said: "*I am making a covenant with you. Before all your people I will do wonders never before done in any nation in all the world. The people you live among will see how awesome the work is that I, the Lord will do for you. Obey what I command you today. I will drive out before you the Amorites, Canaanites, Hittites, Perizzites, Hivites and Jebusites. Be careful not to make a treaty with those who live in the land where you are going, or they will be a snare among you. Break down their altars, smash their sacred stones and cut down their Asherah poles. Do not worship any other god, for the Lord, whose name is Jealous, is a jealous God. Be careful not to make a treaty with those who live in the land; for when they prostitute themselves to their gods and sacrifice to them, they will invite you and you will eat their sacrifices. And when you choose some of their daughters as wives for your sons and those daughters prostitute themselves to their gods, they will lead your sons to do the same. Do not make any idols* (Exodus 34:10-17).

In addition to more commands, Moses was instructed to write the Ten Commandments [1] on two tablets of stone. Then,

---

[1] The Ten Commandments were designed to convict the Israelites of their sins and seek forgiveness. Imagine working in a garden and getting dirt on your hands and face. Looking into a mirror you see the reflection of the dirt on your face. That's what the mirror does, it shows you the dirt. But only water from the faucet can wash it clean. So too, God's commandments revealed the sin that only Jesus' blood could ever wash away.

after another 40 days and nights with God, Moses returned to the Israeli encampment. Moses didn't realize it, but having been in the presence of God changed his visage, his face and hair were radiant white. And when the people saw him they were afraid.

Moses encouraged the people to come near and hear the words of God's covenant. Knowing the people were afraid, when he finished speaking Moses put on a veil to cover his face. And he continued doing so while walking through the camp. However, when Moses entered the tent of meeting[2] to speak with God, he removed the veil.

---

[2] The phrase "tent of meeting" described two different tents. One was the actual tent of the Tabernacle; where inside was the Holy of Holies, a sacred place where God's Shekinah Glory appeared above the Mercy Seat. The other was a portable tent erected by Moses. Before the actual Tabernacle was constructed, Moses pitched this tent some distance away from the Israeli campsite. The separation was intentional. God wanted a private place to speak with Moses. As Moses entered this tent of meeting, a pillar-like cloud descended and remained visible at the tent's entrance while Moses was inside. (Exodus 33:7, 9) After the Tabernacle was built, the phrase "tent of meeting" transitioned to mean the actual Tabernacle.

CHAPTER 6

THE AARONIC PRIESTHOOD

Abraham's descendant, Levi, was chosen by God to be the father of a priestly tribe. When Moses was given God's laws on Mount Sinai, the Levites were identified to be the servants of the Tabernacle. And Moses' brother, Aaron, was chosen by God to become the progenitor of Levite priests.

The High Priest

In the Mosaic Covenant, God ordained an earthly priesthood whose central figure was designated as the High Priest. Before God Almighty that person represented the entire nation of Israel. Being Levites, Aaron's sons were assigned the task of serving as priests in this earthly Tabernacle. As the initial High Priest, Aaron administered the priesthood and acted as a mediator between the nation of Israel and God. He and his sons were responsible for making intercession on behalf of the Israelites. They did so by assisting in the people's offering of various sacrifices. As High Priest, Aaron was allowed once each year to enter the Most Holy Place. On that day, Aaron would present sacrificial blood for himself, and for the people. It was called the Day of Atonement. All of the sacrifices offered in the Tabernacle courtyard just *covered* the sins of the Israelites. Only when Jesus came to "take away the sin of the world," were those sins *removed*.

"For dignity and honor"

The High Priest was outfitted in regal apparel. It comprised of seven different pieces of tailored attire. The garments exalted the office and function of the High Priest, setting him apart from the rest of the priests.

As outlined in Exodus 28:2, Aaron's sacred garments were specifically designed *"for dignity and honor."* His vestments clearly identified him as someone uniquely appointed to serve God. Aaron's layers of clothing began with a white tunic, which was worn next to the skin. The white tunic was symbolic of righteousness. It was a skillfully woven undergarment made out of fine white linen. Though unseen, it was beautifully made and costly to make. Over the tunic Aaron wore a long white garment that hung down to his feet. The other priests wore these same two garments. Over the second tunic, Aaron wore a blue robe. As God's emissary on earth, the blue was symbolic of Aaron's heavenly appointment. Embroidered at the bottom of his blue robe were bells made out of gold, and woven between the bells were pomegranates of blue, purple and scarlet yarn. The blue pomegranates represented heaven, the purple ones royalty, and the scarlet ones, sacrificial blood. The array of colors revealed a future time when Jesus would establish an eternal priesthood. As Aaron performed his priestly duties inside the Tabernacle, the bells on the bottom of his blue robe would jingle. The jingling reminded the people of God's watchful presence.

A beautifully woven sash or belt was made to gird Aaron's robes closely to his body. Over Aaron's blue robe was an ornate short-sleeved jacket consisting of two pieces. It was called an ephod. The jacket reached to his shoulders and down to Aaron's waist, just slightly above his blue robe. It was made out of beaten gold with thin wires interwoven with the finest linen of blue, purple and scarlet. The two pieces were connected by two braided gold chains. The chains strapped over Aaron's shoulders exposing its front and back sides. At the shoulders, two onyx stones (set in gold) were fashioned into the ephod. As a memorial, the names of the twelve tribes of Israel (Jacob) were inscribed on them; six on each stone. Twelve different precious and/or semi-precious stones set in gold were attached to its sacred breastplate which was made out finely twisted gold, blue, purple and scarlet yarn. The pattern of stone placement was four rows with three stones in a row. The first row was comprised of a Sardis stone, a topaz, and an emerald. The second row had a turquoise stone, a sapphire, and a diamond. The third row had a jacinth, an agate, and an amethyst. And in the fourth row, there was a beryl, an onyx, and a jasper stone. When entering the Tabernacle, Aaron ceremoniously carried on his shoulders the weight of the people's sins. Each stone on the breastplate was engraved with the name of one of the twelve tribes. These stones were placed over Aaron's heart where he bore symbolically the nation's judgment. The final apparel crowned his head. It was a turban made out of fine linen with a gold plate attached to its front by a blue cord. Engraved on the plate were the words, "Holiness to the Lord." While Aaron wore the turban those words always appeared on his forehead. While carrying out his duties as High Priest, the words on that plate served as a reminder to do so with utmost reverence.

In Exodus 28:30 Moses was told, "*And you shall put in the breastplate of judgment the Urim and the Thummim, and they shall be over Aaron's heart when he goes in before the Lord. So Aaron shall bear the judgment of the children of Israel over his heart before the Lord continually.*" Though not exactly sure of the physical substance of the Urim and Thummin, they could have been black and white stones. These two items were placed inside a pocket which was designed into the ephod over the heart. The items were used as wordless lots, identifying God's "yes" or "no" to a specific question. If a lot turned up black, God's response was negative. However, if it turned up white, then God's desire was to proceed forward.

The Aaronic Priesthood

At the time of Aaron's and the other priests' consecration, a bull and two rams without blemish were brought to a Brazen Altar (discussed later in Chapter 8) as a blood sacrifice unto God. In addition, a meal offering was presented to God. After washing in a specially designed washbasin called a Laver, Aaron dressed himself in his High Priestly garb. A sacred anointing oil, a blend of spices and olive oil, was then poured over his head as he was announced as the nation's High Priest. Next, with the same special oil, Aaron's sons were anointed as priests. The specially blended oil was used to consecrate Moses' Tent of Meeting, the Ark of the Covenant, the Altar of Burnt Offerings, the Laver, and all of the ancillary accessories and utensils germane to the Tabernacle. During the consecration ceremony, Aaron and all the priests placed their hands on the bull's head confessing their own sins. Then the bull was sacrificed. While the priests were elevated in their position, they were not any better than anyone else. They, too, were sinners in need of God's grace and mercy.

Aaron took a sharp knife and cut the bull's carotid artery. Some of the bull's blood was placed on the Brazen Altar along with the bull's inward parts. Its internal organs were removed and burned on the altar. The bull's carcass was taken outside the Tabernacle area and burned. The bull's demise was considered a sin offering. (Sin offerings, and more, are covered in Chapter 7). According to Exodus 29:35-37 other bulls were to be sacrificed by Aaron and his sons for seven straight days. During this purification ordination, a ram was sacrificed as a burnt offering and its blood applied to the Brazen Altar. It was cut in pieces, and its inward parts washed before the entrails and the entire ram was placed on the altar and burnt. A second ram was killed and some of its blood was applied to Aaron's and his sons' right ear, right thumb, and big toe on the right foot. Figuratively, the blood sanctified the ear to hear God; the hand to assist God in His work; and the foot to walk in the way of God's will. More of its blood was sprinkled around the entire altar and on their priestly garments. The sprinkling of blood testified to the fact that the priests themselves were sinners. As a peace offering, the ram's inward parts, and right thigh, along with a loaf of bread and a wafer, were placed in Aaron's and his sons' hands. Before the Lord, the washed inward parts and bread were waved up and down, and over and back. The washed parts were received back and burnt on the altar as an offering by fire. The animal's breast was reserved as Aaron's portion and he waved it before the Lord. The thigh was waived before the Lord and was given to Aaron and his sons as part of their peace offering. In the new covenant to come, a perfect mediator and high priest would appear. Someone who would shed His own blood.

The New Testament reveals that the Aaronic Priesthood with its High Priest and sacrificial practices was designed to be a sign pointing to Christ. Unlike Aaron, who was only allowed to meet with God once a year, as our eternal High Priest and advocate, Jesus opened the door for all believers to enter the "Holy of Holies," whenever, wherever, and forever. Jesus' sinless sacrifice, made him the perfect and complete sacrifice.

Mysterious Melchizedek

In Genesis Chapter 14, we read where Abram's clan grew and became wealthy in both livestock and gold. Abram had a nephew named Lot. They decided to part ways and Abram gave Lot livestock and land near the town of Sodom. Over time, trouble broke out in the territory where Lot had taken up roots. A battle ensued, and together with his family and all possessions, Lot was taken captive. Abram came to his nephew's aid. Abram armed 300 of his trained men and pursed after the enemy who had taken Lot. They caught up with the enemy forces and prevailed over them. Abram and his forces brought back Lot and his family, plus all of the stolen goods, and the citizenry of Sodom who had been taken as slaves. Then the King of Salem (ancient Jerusalem) named Melchizedek, went out to meet Abram. He brought with him bread and wine so the two of them could enjoy a covenant meal together. The Bible tells us that Melchizedek was a priest of the Most High God and that he blessed Abram. *"Blessed be Abram of the God Most High, Creator of heaven and earth. And praise be to the God Most High, who delivered your enemies into your hand."* In return for the blessing, Abram gave him a tenth of the spoils of war.

The name Melchizedek means *righteous king*. By comparison, in Hebrews 6:19-20 the writer explains that after his resurrection, Jesus became a High Priest *"after the order of Melchizedek."* More is mentioned about this priest in Hebrews 7:1-3. *This Melchizedek was king of Salem and priest of the God Most High. He met Abraham returning from the defeat of the kings and blessed him, and Abraham gave him a tenth of everything. First, the name Melchizedek means "king of righteousness"; then also, "king of Salem" meaning "king of peace." Without father or mother, without genealogy, without beginning of days or end of life, resembling the Son of God, he remains a priest forever.* "King of Righteousness" and "King of Peace" identified Melchizedek as a type of Christ. He had no record of beginning or ending and whose existence is from everlasting to everlasting. Thus Melchizedek personified the very essence of the Son of God.

Mystery Solved

Under the Mosaic Law, only Levites could be priests, and by the Davidic Covenant, only those from the tribe of Judah could be kings. So how did Jesus become both a King and High Priest? Well, we know that Jesus' step-father was of the tribe of Judah, and as a son by adoption, Jesus is rightly a King.

Upon returning to Heaven, Jesus sat down in the right hand of the Father to rule as King over His spiritual kingdom. In the second chapter of Acts, the apostle Peter told an audience in Jerusalem that Jesus was the fulfillment of a covenant promise made to King David. God assured David that He would place one of his descendants on his throne. And God did. When Jesus arose from the dead, He became king of both Heaven and earth.

Daniel's Vision of Jesus as King

In my vision at night I looked, and there before me was one like a son of man coming with the clouds of heaven. He approached the Ancient of Days and was led into his presence. He was given authority, glory and sovereign power; all nations and peoples of every language worshiped him. His dominion is an everlasting dominion that will not pass away, and his kingdom is one that will never be destroyed. Daniel 17:13-14

The Order of Melchizedek

Priests were normally from the tribe of Levi, but Mary wasn't a descendant of Levi. So Jesus must have been from a different priestly order. As the writer of Hebrews explained in Chapters 6 and 7, Jesus was of the order of Melchizedek. Melchizedek pre-dated the Aaronic Priesthood, which indicated that it was lawful for someone to be both a king and a priest of the one true God. So like Melchizedek, Jesus was ordained as a priest apart from the Mosaic Law. But like the Levitical priest, Jesus offered up a blood sacrifice pleasing to God, Himself. And Jesus' ultimate sacrifice on the cross gained eternal redemption for all believers. As High Priest, Jesus was of the order of Melchizedek. The fact that Melchizedek was *"without father or mother, without genealogy, without beginning of days or end of life,"* begs the question, "Was Melchizedek actually the pre-incarnate Son of God?"

CHAPTER 7

THE MOSAIC OFFERINGS

On Mount Sinai, God gave Moses the design for an earthly dwelling referred to as a Tabernacle. It was to be equipped with special furniture and become the home of the Ark of the Covenant. Resting on top of the Ark of the Covenant was a uniquely designed Mercy Seat. Chapter 8 discusses the Tabernacle in significant detail. Outside the Tabernacle, in the courtyard, God instructed Moses to make a Brazen Altar, designed for the burning of sacrifices. And to that end, God gave Moses instructions for the preparation of specific offerings. The sacrificial offerings were intended to draw the Israelites closer to God. And each offering foreshadowed something about God's final offering, His Son, Jesus Christ.

Under the Mosaic Law, five major types of offerings were defined with a sixth (a drink offering) mentioned.
- Sin,
- Trespass
- Burnt

- Meal or Grain
- Drink
- Peace or Communion

The self-explanatory sin and trespass offerings were mandatory offerings. They were created for everyone, including the priests. The other three were voluntary offerings of worship. These were aimed at giving praises back to God. The following chart identifies each type of offering, its required sacrifice, and symbolic reference. It serves as an abridged introduction to the topic.

Mosaic Offerings/Sacrifices		
These offerings covered the sins of the people while providing them a means of worship. The sacrificial animals were symbolic of fully surrendered lives.		
Type	**Sacrifice**	**Symbolic Reference**
Sin Offering	The sin offering dealt with unintentional sins by the priests, or the whole community, or a leader, or a member of the community. Depending on the entity, this sacrifice could be a spotless bull, lamb, goat, turtledove, or pigeon. Sin offerings required the sinner to kill the animal being sacrificed. The priest placed its blood on the horns of the Brazen altar, represented God's strength, granting forgiveness.	The sacrifice transferred the guilt of unintentional sin. Jesus was mankind's guilt bearer and became the ultimate sin offering. As the animal fat dissolved into oil, symbolically it represented the presence of the Holy Spirit. Leviticus 16:8-10
Trespass or Guilt Offering	Trespass offerings dealt with an actual trespass and the guilt brought about by someone's intentional act. The trespass offering required a ram without defect and the sinner was required to make restitution to the injured party. Also, 20% of the amount owed was assessed as a penalty to be paid to the priest.	Symbolic of the payment for intentional sin's deadly consequences. It pointed directly to Jesus' trespass offering on the cross. Leviticus 5:14-19 and 6:1-7; 1 John 1:5-10
Burnt Offerings	Burnt offerings were a voluntary means for an Israelite to commune with God. The offering acknowledged one's sinful nature and that person's desire for a renewed relationship.	Symbolic of Jesus' surrendering to His Father will, and His total dedication to atone for mankind's sins.

Type	Sacrifice	Symbolic Reference
	This offering was either a bull, lamb, goat, turtle dove or a pigeon, and always a male without defect. The person making the sacrifice had to be repentant. Hands were laid on the animal's head as it was dedicated to God. Then the animal's throat was cut by the person and its blood gathered by the priest. The priest sprinkled its blood around the Brazen altar. The animal's cut-up body parts were arranged on the altar, including its head and fat, and burned throughout the night until morning.	Leviticus 1:3-17 Leviticus 6:8-13 2 Corinthians 5:21
Grain or Meal Offerings	A blood sacrifice always preceded a grain offering. Grain offerings included ingredients of fine flour, olive oil and sprinkled frankincense. To become fine flour the grain had to be crushed. If baked or prepared on a griddle, honey or yeast was never to be included. Grain offerings, like all offering, were always to be seasoned with salt. With grain offerings the priest always took a handful of the mixture or unleavened bread and burned it on the Brazen altar. With this holy offering some of the bread and roasted animal was given to the priest and the Israelite family offering the sacrifice.	The crushing of grain was symbolic of Jesus, who knew no sin, crushing the head of Satan. And the frankincense symbolic of the aroma received by God of His Son's loving sacrifice. The meal offering became symbolic of the believer's oneness with Christ in the Passover Meal. Leviticus 2:1-14 Hebrews 10:5-10 Luke 22:17-23
Drink Offerings	Burnt and grain offerings also included drink offerings. Certain amounts of wine were to be poured over the sacrifices placed on the Brazen altar.	Metaphorically the pouring out of the drink offering represented Jesus' blood spilled out on the cross.
Peace or Fellowship Offerings This sacrifice always included a meal offering afterwards	The peace offering could be either a male of female animal without defect. At the entrance of the Tent of Meeting hands were laid on its head before it was slain. Its blood was sprinkled on the Brazen altar by a priest. The fat around the animal's internal organs including the kidneys and liver were removed along with the kidneys. These parts were burnt above the flesh sacrifice. Then a meal offering was presented. Afterwards the priest and Israelite ate a meal together, representing the forgiven sinner and God fellowshipping.	Symbolic of Christ's body and blood as well as the descending Holy Spirit in the fat transformed into oil. Together with a meal and drink offering, the Peace Offering represented the sacrament of Holy Communion. Leviticus 3:1-17 Judges 20:26 Ephesians 2:14-18

Sin Offerings

Sin offerings were for unintentional sins. For this offering, sacrificed animals had to be without defects; a spotless bull, lamb, goat, turtledove, or pigeon. All of which foreshadowed the "spotless" Lamb of God. The animal was brought to the altar where the sinner laid hands on its head, symbolically transferring unintentional sins onto the animal. Then the animal's carotid artery was slashed. Close by, a priest collected its blood, sprinkling some of it on the horns of a specially designed Brazen Altar. The horns represented God's strength, and his grace to forgive sins. While being applied to the horns on the altar, the life in the blood shouted out to God for forgiveness. The rest of its blood was poured out at the altar's base. The carcass and altar ashes were always removed to a place outside the camp. This action emphasized God's revulsion and repugnance to sin, and emphsized the separtion it produced. Other than a portion given to the priest for his services, the entire animal was burnt as the sin offering.

The Final Sin Offering

In time, the final sin offering was Jesus's sacrifice on the cross. His shed blood reconciled repentant sinners to God. Romans 6:6 reminds us, *"For we know that our old self was crucified with him so that the body ruled by sin might be done away with, that we should no longer be slaves to sin."*

The Trespass Offering

The trespass offering was personal. It dealt with an individual's intentional sins, and if someone was harmed by the party, restitution was required. The person placed his hands on the head of a ram, confessing his sins. After the animal was slain, the priest captured its blood, offering it up with the fat from the animal's internal organs. Back and forth over the burning sacrifice the animal's blood was sprinkled by the priest. The trespass offering was primarily about making reparations; and atoning sacrifice before God, and restitution to man. With the trespass offering, the priest was allowed to keep and eat the rest of the roasted, animal sacrifice.

Jesus as the Trespass Offering

In the new covenant, Jesus became the repentant sinner's Trespass Offering. On Himself, Jesus took on all of the sins of repentant sinners, including those in the future they would commit. This was something the blood of bulls and goats could never do. For more understanding, read Hebrews chapters nine and ten.

The Apostle Paul wrote in Colossians 2:13-14, "*When you were dead in your sins and in the uncircumcision of your flesh, God made you alive with Christ. He forgave us all our sins, having canceled the charge of our legal indebtedness, which stood against us and condemned us; he has taken it away, nailing it to the cross.*" And 1 John 1:6-9 we are reminded that through the blood of Jesus, "*if we confess our sins, that God is faithful and just, and will forgive our sins, cleaning us from all unrighteousness.*"

Burnt Offerings followed by Grain Offerings

The first recorded burnt offering occurred when Noah offered up a sacrifice after the flood (Genesis 8:20). And then again when God ordered Abraham to offer up Isaac as a burnt offering (Genesis 22:2). Burnt offerings were dialoged in Exodus 10:24-26 as Pharaoh and Moses discussed letting God's people go. *"Then Pharaoh summoned Moses and said, 'Go, worship the LORD. Even your women and children may go with you; only leave your flocks and herds behind.' But Moses said, 'You must allow us to have sacrifices and burnt offerings to present to the Lord our God. Our livestock too must go with us; not a hoof is to be left behind. We have to use some of them in worshiping the Lord our God, and until we get there we will not know what we are to use to worship the Lord."*

Burnt offerings were a voluntary means for the Israelites to commune with God. A person could present to God a burnt offering anytime. The offering acknowledged one's sinful nature and that person's desire for a renewed relationship. Depending on a person's economic position, the offering could be a spotless bull, lamb, goat, turtle dove or a pigeon. Burnt Offerings were always males without defects brought into the Tabernacle courtyard by the sinner.

Standing on the north side of the brazen altar, a transgressor's hands were placed on an animal's head as its throat was cut. A priest captured its blood and then sprinkled or splashed it around and about the altar. The priest then skinned the sacrifice, removing its internal organs, and legs, washing them with water. Then, with the exception of their skin which was given to the priest for his help, the burnt offering remained on the altar all night until completely charred, i.e., its head, internal fat, washed legs, internal organs, and remaining body. If a bird was used its head was twisted off, blood drained and feathers removed. The bird was then burnt on the altar.

The Israelite was symbolically giving himself completely back to God, holding nothing back. And the smoke arising from the altar of sacrifice became a sweet aroma unto God. Immediately following the Burnt Offering was a Grain or Meal Offering.

Jesus as the Ultimate Burnt Offering

The ultimate fulfillment of this offering took place at Calvary. Jesus' body was completely consumed as he gave up his Spirit on the cross. In the New Covenant, Jesus became the Father's burnt offering to mankind. We read in Ephesians 5:1-2, *"Follow God's example, therefore, as dearly loved children and walk in the way of love, just as Christ loved us and gave himself up for us as a fragrant offering and sacrifice to God."*

Grain or Meal Offerings

Grain offering ingredients included the finest flour, olive oil, and incense. If baked or prepared on a griddle, olive oil was to be added, but never honey or yeast. Grain offerings, like all offerings, were to be seasoned with salt. (Salt Covenants are covered in Chapter 11.) With Grain Offerings, the priest always took a memorial portion of the grain or bread and burned it on the altar. The rest of the offering belonged to Aaron and his sons.

A blood sacrifice always preceded a meal offering. This offering was made with fine flour, mingled with olive oil. For seasoning, salt and frankincense was added. To become fine flour the grain had to be crushed. This offering could be in raw form or baked, or fried, or roasted. It was an Israelite's way of saying, "I'm offering my whole life to you." The meal offering was given to a priest who burned a handful back to God. Understood was that the handful represented the whole. The remainder of the meal offering was given to the priest and his family.

As the true bread, Jesus walked in complete obedience with the Father. Through His death, burial and resurrection, Jesus fulfilled the meal offering as the true bread of life. There was no leaven in His life, only a sweet fragrance unto the Father. And like the oil, Jesus' life was filled with the Holy Spirit. When Jesus was baptized, the heavens opened and the Spirit of God descended on Jesus like a dove.

Drink Offerings

Right after God changed Jacob's name to Israel, Jacob is mentioned as pouring out a drink offering on an altar of some sort (Genesis 35:14). In Exodus 29:40-41 Moses received instructions that burnt and grain offerings also included drink offerings. Wine was to be poured over the sacrifices placed on the altar of fire. The requirement was a quart of wine for each lamb; 1 1/3 quarts for each ram, and two quarts of wine for each bull (Numbers 15). The collective altar offering of an animal, grain, oil and wine created a unique aroma pleasing to the Lord. Literally, the person making the offering was preparing a meal for God. But metaphorically, the pouring out of the drink offering represented Jesus' future blood spilled on the cross. When Jesus instituted the New Covenant, he picked up a cup of wine and said, *"This cup which is poured out for you is the new covenant in My blood."* While hanging on the cross, Jesus' blood literally poured out when the soldier pierced His side with a spear, thus fulfilling the requirement of a drink offering.

Peace or Fellowship Offerings

All of the offerings pointed to this final offering known as a peace offering. The peace offering was a celebration knowing that one was in covenant with God. Like the other offerings, hands were laid on an animal's head and sins confessed before the animal's throat was cut. The person offering this animal's blood was responsible for cutting the animal's throat. The priests captured its blood, sprinkling it all around and upon the altar. The animal's fat was removed and burnt on the altar. With the help of the priest, two parts of the animal sacrifice were offered up to God; the breast which represented the heart of man, and the right shoulder which represented one's strength. The body parts were held by the Israelite as the priest placed his hands under the Israelite's hands. The sacrifice, like the image of a cross, was raised up and then sideways before God. After being dedicated to God, the sacrifice was given back to the sinner and baked on the altar. The High Priest was given the breast, and the right shoulder given to the assisting priest. In addition to the animal sacrifice, a meal offering of unleavened bread, as well as a few loaves of leavened bread, were brought by the Israelite to the ceremony. With the ceremony complete, the remaining sacrifice that was baked on the brazen altar, together with the loaves of bread, were eaten in the Tabernacle courtyard by the family. Ceremoniously, the parties to this covenant meal became one with God. He was in them, and now they were in Him.

Jesus' Peace

In the new covenant, Jesus became a peace offering. After His resurrection, the heart and strength of God returned to His Son. Christians now receive the priestly portion of the sacrifice in the form of the Holy Spirit. As our High Priest, Jesus bears over His heart and shoulders the names of all repentant believers.

Shalom

Jesus reminded His followers in John 14:27, "*Peace I leave with you; my peace I give you. I do not give to you as the world gives. Do not let your hearts be troubled and do not be afraid.*" The interpretation of this godly kind of peace is, "that which comes from lacking nothing." It is a complete peace.

Salaam Alacum is an Arabic expression covenant friends use. It means, "How is your peace? Are you lacking anything?" If the return answer is that the person lacks something, it is the asking party's responsibility to give (if possible) whatever is lacking to him. After the restoration of salaam, the peace that comes from lacking nothing is restored.

The Peace found in David's 23rd Psalm

In the 23rd Psalm, David begins, "*The Lord is my shepherd.*" As David cared for his flocks, so the Lord cared for David. "*I shall not want*" indicated that nothing else was needed, their covenant relationship was complete. If asked by God, "Salaam Alacum?" David would have responded, "Lord, I am lacking nothing." In fact, David said, "*the Lord is my Shepherd, I shall not want.*" The apostle Paul wrote in Philippians 4:19, "*And my God will meet all your needs according to the riches of his glory in Christ Jesus.*" This passage reflects that God desires to provide for His sheep's need, and that's level one. Level two is this: even wants can be provided by God.

Next, David revealed in this Psalm, "*He makes me lie down in green pastures; he leads me beside the still waters.*" As David's Good Shepherd, the Lord led him to places of restful intimacy. David loved the Lord and that is who he served. God was his rock. David continued, "*He restores my soul, He leads me in the paths of righteousness for His name's sake.*" The word restore comes from the root word shaleem which means to make whole all my soul. In other words, whatever is lacking, you will lack no more. To David, the Lord was his Jehovah Jireh, his provider.

As shepherd, and leader of the people, David had anxiety issues. When his soul needed refreshing, David prayed and sang songs unto his Lord. David leaned on God and relied on Him for salaam.

In verse four of this Psalm, David shared insight into his faith. *"Yea, though I walk through the valley of the shadow of death, I will fear no evil for you are with me; your rod and staff, they comfort me."* Shepherds used rods or clubs to defend the sheep from wild prey. In order to get to a sheep, a wild animal had to first get through David. As a shepherd, David's staff had a crook. It was used to gently guide and direct the path of an errant sheep. To David, the Lord's staff afforded him protection as well as correction. During times of testing, walking through the valley of shadow of death was only necessary to reach the other side. If God is your Shepherd, what is there to fear? Deep in his heart, David knew there wasn't anything capable getting past his Shepherd.

Then David makes a most fascinating statement, *"You prepare a table before me in the presence of my enemies; you anoint my head with oil; My cup runs over."* David rested in the arms of the Good Shepherd. Even when approaching enemies were in direct pursuit, he wasn't fazed. The phrase, *"You prepare a table before me in the presence of my enemies,"* can be interpreted metaphorically as sitting down with God, enjoying a covenant meal. Once the enemy recognized David's covenant partner, the awesome God of Israel, they recognized their futility and turned away.

In Middle East communities it is common to see large tents erected in the streets. Inside and outside of the tents, people are seen eating and dancing, celebrating the observance of a blood covenant ceremony. The celebration takes place in an open environment because the covenant makers want their enemies to see their strength. Should an enemy tangle with one covenant partner, the enemy can expect to receive the wrath from the other. Ask yourself, "Is God your covenant partner?"

CHAPTER 8

THE EARTHLY TABERNACLE

On Mount Sinai, God gave Moses special design instructions for constructing and furnishing an earthly Tabernacle. Looking back from the New Testament, God's divine plan revealed the coming of a Savior. The Tabernacle was to be a hallowed place where God would communicate with the Israelites through Moses and God's appointed High Priest, Aaron. Surrounding God's Tabernacle would be myriads of tents housing the various tribes of Israel. Nestled closely around the Tabernacle itself, God wanted a particular Jewish tribe known as the Levites. The Levites were appointed by God as Israel's priests. And as such, they were assigned daily duties inside the Tabernacle area.

The Tabernacle

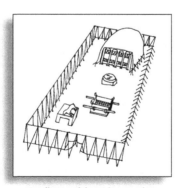

God's Earthly Tabernacle

God gave Moses the dimensions of the enclosed area. The area of the Tabernacle was to be 150 feet by 75 feet. Curtains, approximately 8 feet in height, comprised its perimeter. The entrance or gate into the sacred area was located on its eastside. The entry drape was to be fashioned out of finely twisted blue, purple and scarlet linen. And it was the only way to get to God. In the New Testament, Jesus remarked, *"I am the way and the truth and the life. No one comes to the Father except through me."*

The Brazen Altar

Upon entering the courtyard of this earthly tabernacle one could see a large Brazen Altar. Animals were sacrificed unto the Lord on that altar. The altar was constructed of wood and entirely overladen in brass. It featured animal horns on each of its four corners. As a sweet smelling savor unto the Lord, various types of offerings were brought to the priests to be sacrificed.

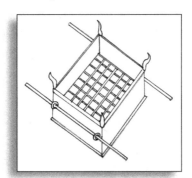

Brazen Altar for Sacrificed Animals

In order to receive penance, the Israelites were allowed to enter the outer court of the Tabernacle with their animal sacrifices. However, only Israelites with acceptable sacrifices were allowed to enter. In the outer court animals were slain and burnt on this altar of sacrifice. This was God's method for penitence, not forgiveness. As explained in Leviticus 17:11, *"for the life of a creature is in the blood, and I have given it to you to make atonement for yourselves on the altar; it is the blood that makes atonement for one's life."* Absolution for sin would take place on the cross at Calvary.

It was by God's grace that He allowed the people's sins to be cast on the animals' heads. Their sin was then burned on a brazen altar. As creatures without souls, these animals were sinless offerings. In the New Covenant, *"God made Jesus who had no sin to be sin for us, so that in him we might become the righteousness of God."* 2 Corinthians 5:21. The Brazen (Brass) Altar personified Jesus' sacrifice on the cross where man's sins were completely forgiven.

Whenever the Brazen Altar had to be moved, designed rings were used for poles to slip in them. Priests were assigned the task of carrying the altar on their shoulders. This was God's command.

The Laver

In the courtyard, west of the Brazen Altar, was a wash basin referred to as a Laver. It was made of polished brass and used for ceremonial cleansing. The priests used the laver to wash their hands and feet before entering the Tabernacle.

In the New Testament, Jesus told Nicodemus, *"except a man be born of water and spirit, he cannot enter the kingdom of God."*

We know that in the New Covenant, Jesus' righteousness became ascribed to all believers. So, believers could approach God through Jesus as their High Priest, appearing both clean and righteous. I John 1:9 says, *"If we confess our sins, he is faithful and just to forgive us our sins, and to cleanse us from all unrighteousness."*

The Actual Tabernacle

The Tabernacle was built and located in the back portion of the courtyard. It was a place where only priests were allowed. Goat hair skins and the skins of badgers covered its exterior. Underneath these exterior skins were ram skins dyed red. Observing from the outside, the Tabernacle seemed unassuming. But looking up from the inside at the red dyed ram skins were appealing. By comparison, as a carpenter from Nazareth, Jesus' persona was unassuming. But Jesus certainly wasn't unassuming. This red color applied to the ram skins foreshadowed Jesus' precious blood.

Inside the tented Tabernacle was a Holy Place, and further back, a room known as the Holy of Holies. In that room, only the High Priest (Aaron) was allowed to enter, and then only once a year. Inside this Holy of Holies, God's Shekinah Glory manifested itself.

When entering the Tabernacle, the priests passed through a veil made of blue, purple and scarlet linen. Behind this initial veil was the Holy Place. Inside to the south was a candlestick with seven branches, all made of pure gold. Directly across from the candlestick was a table where loaves of showbread were placed. And then, directly west of those items was an Altar of Incense.

The golden candlestick, or menorah, had a middle branch that fed olive oil to the other six branches. These six branches had numerous small almond shaped cups that held small amounts of olive oil as its power source. The candlestick provided light where no natural light could penetrate. As Jesus said, "*I am the light of the world.*" The candlestick symbolically represented God. Its central shaft pointing to the Son of God and the oil flowing through and filling the six branches foreshadowed the indwelling of the Holy Spirit. Each morning and at twilight, Aaron was required to tend to the candles.

On the north side of the Holy Place, directly across from the candlestick, was a rectangular table overlaid in pure gold called the Table of Showbread. On it sat twelve loaves of bread, which represented Israel's twelve different tribes. The loaves were placed there in two piles of six apiece. Each Sabbath the old loaves were replaced with new loaves. Next to the loaves were trays and vessels containing wine. After Aaron exchanged the loaves each week, he and his sons ate the removed bread and drank of the wine.

I Am the Bread of Life

Jesus' announced in John 6:51-58 that He was the bread of life. "*I am the living bread that came down from heaven. Whoever eats this bread will live forever. This bread is my flesh, which I will give for the life of the world.*" *Then the Jews began to argue sharply among themselves, "How can this man give us his flesh to eat?" Jesus said to them, "Very truly I tell you, unless you eat the flesh of the*

Son of Man and drink his blood, you have no life in you. Whoever eats my flesh and drinks my blood has eternal life, and I will raise them up at the last day. For my flesh is real food and my blood is real drink. Whoever eats my flesh and drinks my blood remains in me, and I in them. Just as the living Father sent me and I live because of the Father, so the one who feeds on me will live because of me. This is the bread that came down from heaven. Your ancestors ate manna and died, but whoever feeds on this bread will live forever."

Entering the Holy of Holies

Deep inside the Holy area was a thick curtain made of intertwined fine linen and purple, blue and scarlet yarn. Embroidered on the curtain were figures of cherubim. The veil separated the Holy area from the most holy area, the Holy of Holies. And centered directly in front of the veil was an Altar of Incense. This was a small square table with four horns, one on each corner. It, too, was covered in pure gold. Aaron was required to place burning coals on the altar before sprinkling the coals with incense. Symbolic of prayers, the reaction emitted a fragrant cloud of smoke lifted up before God. Only incense was allowed to be burned on this altar, with one exception. On the Day of Atonement (fully discussed in Chapter 11) the high priest was allowed to apply blood on that altar's horns.

Inside the Holy of Holies was a single piece of furniture, the Ark of the Covenant. The Ark was a chest with an attached lid referred to as The Mercy Seat. This was God's earthly throne. Replicas of cherubim were attached to each end of the Mercy Seat's cover.

Their outstretched wings met at the middle of the lid. Just above the Mercy Seat, between the cherubim, God manifested Himself in a bright light known as His Shekinah glory. Placed inside the Ark were three objects:

- Aaron's rod that budded with almonds
- A small pot of manna
- The stone tablets of God's Ten Commandments

Aaron's Rod that Budded

After Aaron was designated by God to be the Israelites' High Priest, jealousy arose among some the Levites. God wasn't pleased and put a stop to their cantankerous reaction. Those challenging God's decision were told to lay down staffs of wood to see which one budded. In Numbers 17:1-12 the Lord said to Moses, "*Speak to the Israelites and get twelve staffs from them, one from the leader of each of their ancestral tribes. Write the name of each man on his staff. On the staff of Levi write Aaron's name, for there must be one staff for the head of each ancestral tribe. Place them in the tent of meeting in front of the Ark of the Covenant law, where I meet with you. The staff belonging to the man I choose will sprout, and I will rid myself of this constant grumbling against you by the Israelites.*" *So Moses spoke to the Israelites, and their leaders gave him twelve staffs, one for the leader of each of their ancestral tribes, and Aaron's staff was among them. Moses placed the staffs before the Lord in the tent of the covenant law. The next day Moses entered the tent and saw that Aaron's staff, which represented the tribe of Levi, had not*

only sprouted but had budded, blossomed and produced almonds.
Then Moses brought out all the staffs from the LORD's presence to
all the Israelites. They looked at them, and each of the leaders took
his own staff. The Lord said to Moses, "Put back Aaron's staff in front
of the Ark of the Covenant law, to be kept as a sign to the rebellious.
This will put an end to their grumbling against me, so that they will
not die." Moses did just as the Lord commanded him.

Aaron's rod that budded was placed inside the Ark of the
Covenant. It served as a reminder of the indignant grumbling that
needed forgiveness and mercy.

The Pot of Manna

Like Jesus, manna was unleavened bread sent from heaven by
God to sustain His people. But it, too, became a bone of conten-
tion. *In the desert the whole community grumbled against Moses*
and Aaron. The Israelites said to them, "If only we had died by the
Lord's hand in Egypt! There we sat around pots of meat and ate all
the food we wanted, but you have brought us out into this desert to
starve this entire assembly to death." Then the Lord said to Moses, "I
will rain down bread from heaven for you. The people are to go out
each day and gather enough for that day. In this way I will test them
and see whether they will follow my instructions."

The manna inside the Ark was a constant reminder of the contentious behavior that looked to God for mercy. It also served as a
reminder of God's provision.

The Tablets of Stone

God's Ten Commandments were placed inside the Ark as a constant reminder of the Israelites' sinful nature, readily identifying their need for a personal Savior. God's righteous bar was set too high for the people to keep God's commandments. Instead, the people depended on the Ark's blood-stained Mercy Seat to change judgment to mercy.

The Torn Veil in the Temple at Jerusalem

Just before Jesus died on the cross, he cried out with a loud voice. Simultaneously, the massive thick curtain in the Jerusalem temple, which allowed the High Priest access to the Holy of Holies, was torn in half from the top to the bottom. That veil was believed to have been about 60 feet in height, close to 30 feet in width and four inches thick. Nobody, except God, had the strength to tear that veil. With the tearing of the veil, God announced symbolically that Jesus' broken body had opened the way for Jesus to approach the Father directly on every believer's behalf. As our High Priest, Jesus entered the presence of the Father with the incense of the saints. As told in the Hebrews 9:12, "*He did not enter (Heaven) by means of the blood of goats and calves; but he entered the Most Holy Place once for all by his own blood, thus obtaining eternal redemption.*"

Jesus Our High Priest

As noted previously, except for the High Priest, no priest was allowed to stand directly before God's presence. Aaron was allowed to approach God but only on the Day of Atonement. We read in Hebrews 9:7, *"But only the high priest entered the inner room, and that only once a year, and never without blood, which he offered for himself and for the sins the people had committed in ignorance."* Aaron was a sinner. As such, he was required to offer up sacrifices for himself before offering them up for the nation of Israel. When the veil in the Jerusalem temple was torn, Jesus became our eternal High Priest. No longer was the Aaronic Priesthood necessary. Being sinless, Jesus opened the door to eternal salvation and direct fellowship with God. Hebrews 10:19-22 reminds us, *"Therefore, brothers, since we have confidence to enter the Most Holy Place by the blood of Jesus, by a new and living way opened for us through the curtain, that is, his body…let us draw near to God with a sincere heart in full assurance of faith."*

When Jesus became mankind's High Priest, God moved out of His earthly tabernacle, never again to reside in an Old Covenant temple built with hands. Christ became every believer's eternal High Priest, through whom the faithful are allowed to enter the Holy of Holies. Through Jesus' death, all barriers between God and man were removed.

CHAPTER 9

GOD'S DESIGNATED COVENANT FEASTS

On Mount Sinai the Lord told Moses that the Sabbath day was to be continually a day of rest for His chosen people. And that every year the people were to observe certain feasts. Those feasts were Passover and the Festival of Unleavened Bread, the Feast of First Fruits and Wave Loaves, the Feast or Festival of Trumpets, the Day of Atonement, and the Feast of Tabernacles.

The following chart identifies each feast, the ceremony involved and its fulfillment in Jesus Christ.

Mosaic Feasts			
Old Testament Name	**Hebrew Name**	**Ceremony**	**Fulfillment**
Sabbath	Shabbat	The Jewish Sabbath was a day of rest. It was a time to refrain from any strenuous work. It began on Friday night just before sunset and lasted until the stars appeared on Saturday night. Candle lightings,	Jesus is the believer's rest. In Matthew 11:28, Jesus said, "Come to me, all you who are weary and burdened, and I will give you rest. Take my yoke upon you and learn from me,

Old Testament Name	Hebrew Name	Ceremony	Fulfillment
Sabbath	Shabbat	prayers, special meals, and recited blessings comprised the Shabbat ceremony.	for I am gentle and humble in heart, and you will find rest for your souls. For my yoke is easy and my burden is light."
Feast of Passover	Pesach	The Passover Seder began on the 14th day of Jewish month of Nisan. This was a perpetual memorial celebrating the Israelites deliverance from slavery in Egypt. The Seder meal included unleavened bread and bitter herbs. In Egypt a lamb or goat without blemish was chosen on the 10th day of that month and slain on the 14th. Its blood was sprinkled on the doorposts and lintels so the angel of death would pass over.	Jesus died during Passover and became the Passover lamb without blemish. His blood was shed on the doorposts of the cross both horizontally and vertically, delivering mankind from the bondage of sin. This celebrated feast is the precursor to the Lord's Supper as outlined in the New Testament.
Feast of Unleavened Bread and Feast of First Fruits	Matzot and Bikkurim	Immediately following Passover, from the 15th to the 21st day of Nisan, sin, burnt, grain and drink offerings were made. For seven days, all leaven was removed. On the 2nd day of the feast (the 16th), the first sheaf of the barley harvest was waved before God. Then again on the 21st day, a barley sheaf from the fall harvest was offered up again, thanking God for His provision.	Jesus is the bread of life that came down from heaven. His resurrection occurred during first fruits. Jesus' crucifixion purged all leaven committed by mankind. Like the first sheaf waved before God, Jesus was the first fruit of those risen from the dead. See 1 Corinthians 15:23.
Pentecost or Festival of Weeks or Feast of Wave Loaves	Shavuot	The Feast of Wave Loaves took place at harvest time, exactly seven weeks and a day after First Fruits. Sin, burnt, grain and drink offerings were made. But this meal offering of "two wave loaves" was quite different because these loaves were baked with leaven.	Exactly 50 days (Pente) after Passover, the Holy Spirit (fine flour) came to reside inside both the sinful (leaven) Jew and Gentile. The Holy Spirit wrote God's laws on the believer's heart. See Jeremiah 31:33.

Old Testament Name	Hebrew Name	Ceremony	Fulfillment
Feast of Trumpets	Rosh Hashanah	This feast celebrated the new year on the 1st day of Tishri. The celebration was announced by a priest blowing a ram's horn (shofar). Animals were sacrificed as burnt offerings and flour mingled with oil was given as a meal offering unto the Lord. Sin was confessed for ten days.	This feast celebrated the new year and represented a time in the future when trumpets would signal the arrival of Jesus' second advent. This will be a time when all of Israel will return and inherit its promised land.
The Day of Atonement	Yom Kippur	This is the most solemn holy day on the Jewish calendar. Each year on the 10th day of Tishri the entire nation of Israel fasted. In addition to the regular daily offerings, a bull was offered as a sin offering, and a ram was sacrificed as a burnt offering for the priest; for the people, two goats were offered as sin offerings; One was sacrificed and its blood sprinkled on the Ark of the Covenant and the other released as a scape goat. The blood sprinkled on the Ark, ritually appeased the ire of God for another year. The second goat took the sins of the people into the wasteland where they were became unattached to the people and forgotten.	On Good Friday Jesus became the ultimate sin offering, atoning for mankind's sins. And simultaneously Jesus became mankind's scape goat because Jesus took away the sins of the world. Jesus is now every believer's High Priest and King.
Feast of Tabernacles or In-gatherings (Known as In-gatherings because it coincided with the end of the harvest season.)	Sukkot	During the fall harvest, this seven day Feast of Tabernacles was celebrated beginning on the 15th day of Tishra. It commemorated the Israelites living in tents during the Exodus and God dwelling with them. During this feast booths were constructed out of tree limbs and the people lived in them for seven days. During the feast period grain/meal offerings were required.	One of God's many names is Jehovah-Jireh, meaning that the God dwelling with us is our provider. As our provider, Jesus Christ is more than enough. It was representative too of a future time when God's people will be gathered to dwell with Jesus forever.

The Shabbat (Sabbath)

Shabbat is celebrated on the seventh day of the week and is Judaism's day of rest. It is a celebrated remembrance of God's resting after creation and the Israelites deliverance from bondage in Egypt. Shabbat is observed a few minutes before sunset on Friday. It is ushered in by the lighting of candles and the reciting of a blessing. The blessing is recited over that evening's meal and a second blessing is made over two special loaves of Jewish bread called challah. According to Exodus 16:22-26, the two loaves memorialized the double portion of manna allowed to be taken in the wilderness for eating on the Sabbath. Just before the bread is broken into smaller pieces and passed to family members, salt is sprinkled over the entire loaf. The Shabbat memorializes the "salt covenant." In one respect, the family's table becomes a makeshift altar. The covenant meal concludes the following evening with a special blessing called the Havdalah.

The Passover's Significance in the New Covenant

The annual Passover Feast celebrated the Israelites deliverance from slavery in Egypt. On the first day of the feast they were to do no work. And for the next seven days, they were to eat unleavened bread and offer food offerings unto the Lord. On the following Sabbath they were to conduct a sacred assembly and refrain from doing any regular work.

The Passover Feast foreshadowed Jesus' sacrifice on the cross. The Last Supper was held on a Thursday, during Passover week.

On that day Jesus shared a Passover meal with His disciples. Luke 22:14 -20 tells us, *"When the hour came, Jesus and his apostles reclined at the table. And he said to them, 'I have eagerly desired to eat this Passover with you before I suffer. For I tell you, I will not eat it again until it finds fulfillment in the kingdom of God.' After taking the cup, he gave thanks and said, 'Take this and divide it among you. For I tell you I will not drink again from the fruit of the vine until the kingdom of God comes.' And he took bread, gave thanks and broke it, and gave it to them, saying, 'This is my body given for you; do this in remembrance of me.' In the same way, after the supper he took the cup, saying, 'This cup is the new covenant in my blood, which is poured out for you.'"*

Then after the events which led up to Jesus' crucifixion, Jesus gave up His Spirit, and by the hand of God, the massive veil in the temple split from bottom, up. God's action revealed that earthly high priests would no longer be necessary. As High Priest, Jesus' shed blood became the perfect sacrifice, and He became the way to salvation. Jesus carried His own blood into the true Holy of Holies, where God declared mankind's sins dealt with, never to be remembered again. This action by the Father and the Son, ushered in the Covenant of Redemption. As our High Priest, Jesus offered His own blood as a final and complete sacrifice, atoning for man's sins; past, present, and future.

Communion

The eating of the bread, and drinking of the wine during communion allows Christians everywhere to share in all the blessings of God's covenant with His Son, especially the forgiveness of sin.

Holy Communion – the New Covenant in Jesus Blood

Communion is a sacred sacrament, serving as a vivid reminder of Jesus' ultimate sacrifice on the cross. It should always be received with a humble and repentant heart. The doctrine of transubstantiation suggests that Christ's body and blood become present in the form of the wafer and wine. As covenant partners, all believers should recognize that they, like the disciples, are breaking bread with Jesus. What happens during the covenant meal is most holy. God is placing Himself inside the believer and the believer is placing himself or herself inside Jesus. In other words, "everything that He is, becomes me; and everything I am, He is." The Apostle Paul writes in I Corinthians 10:15-16, *"Is not the cup of thanksgiving for which we give thanks a participation in the blood of Christ? And is not the bread that we break a participation in the body of Christ?"*

In preparation for the receiving of the memorial meal, these words of remembrance are used; *"Our Lord Jesus Christ, on the night when He was betrayed, took bread, and when he had given thanks, he broke it and gave it to his disciples and said, 'Take; eat; this is my body, given for you. This do in remembrance of me.' In the same way, also, He took the cup after supper, and when He had given thanks, He gave it to them saying, 'Drink of it all of you. This cup is the New Testament in My Blood, shed for you for the forgiveness of sins. This do as often as you drink it, in remembrance of Me.'* Thanks be to God.

The Wedding Cake

To declare a covenant's existence, its partners often shared a meal together. The covenant representatives feed each other from the same bread, and partake of drinking out of the same wine goblet. It is like the parties are saying to each other, *"the bread and wine are symbolic of my body and blood which I'm putting in you. Now I am in you and you are in me. We are now one in this covenant relationship."* In a contemporary marriage celebration, the eating of cake is symbolic of this same exchanged vow. The groom extends his hand and places a piece of cake inside his bride's mouth. Simultaneously the bride places a piece of cake inside her husband's mouth. By sharing the covenant meal this way, the couple are saying to each other, "I am putting all of me in you, and you are putting all of you in me. And therefore, all that's mine is yours, and all that's yours is mine."

Warning

The apostle Paul warned the new Christians at Corinth not

to take communion lightly. Always remember, this covenant meal cost Jesus His life! Out of deep gratitude focused hearts are essential. We read in 1 Corinthians 11:25- 29, *"In the same way, after supper he took the cup, saying, 'this cup is the new covenant in my blood; do this, whenever you drink it, in remembrance of me.' For whenever you eat this bread and drink this cup, you proclaim the Lord's death until he comes. So then, whoever eats the bread or drinks the cup of the Lord in an unworthy manner will be guilty of sinning against the body and blood of the Lord. Everyone ought to examine themselves before they eat of the bread and drink from the cup. For those who eat and drink without discerning the body of Christ eat and drink judgment on themselves."*

Feast of Unleavened Bread and First Fruits

Immediately following Passover, from the 15th to the 21st day of Nisan, was the Feast of Unleavened Bread and First Fruits. On the 16th day, a sheaf from the first barley harvest was waved, instead of being burnt on the Altar of sacrifice. Next, a one-year old male lamb without blemish was sacrificed as a burnt offering. In addition, a loaf of unleavened bread made with fine flour, mixed with oil, was offered as a meal offering. On the 21st day, a priest took another barley sheaf, representing the first fruits of the harvest, and offered it up to God, thanking God for His provision.

Feast of Wave Loaves

Exactly 50 days after the Feast of First Fruits, a new meal offering was required. This was known as the Feast of Wave Loaves.

As noted in Leviticus 23:17, during this feast something strange took place. *"From wherever you live, bring two loaves made of two-tenths of an ephah of the finest flour, baked with yeast, as a wave offering of first fruits to the Lord."* What was strange? The yeast! Yeast in the Bible always represented sin. Notice in 1 Corinthians 5:7-8, *"Get rid of the old yeast, so that you may be a new unleavened batch—as you really are. For Christ, our Passover lamb, has been sacrificed. Therefore let us keep the Festival, not with the old bread leavened with malice and wickedness, but with the unleavened bread of sincerity and truth."* Adding yeast was extremely odd because ceremonial bread was always unleavened. Therefore, mixing the finest flour with yeast was most unusual.

This festive ritual required the offering of several animals, one for a sin offering, and two first-year lambs for a peace offering. The peace offering and leaven loaves were waved by a priest before God. The mystery behind the Feasts of First Fruits and Wave Loaves became manifest after Jesus ascended to His Father.

This first fruits offering foreshadowed Jesus' resurrection. The Apostle Paul wrote about the resurrection of the dead in 1 Corinthians 15:23 and identified Christ as being the first fruit, *"But each in turn: Christ, the first fruits; then, when he comes, those who belong to him."* The Feast of Wave Loaves was held exactly 50 days after the Feast of First Fruits. The 50 days paralleled exactly the same number of days from Christ's resurrection to the day of Pentecost.

Spiritual Wave Loaves

After Jesus' resurrection, the disciples were in Jerusalem. Jesus had told them to wait there for an anointing, so they were waiting. Coming from Galilee, a few of the disciples were probably uneasy about being in the city because they were vulnerable to assault. But as commanded, they waited in Jerusalem patiently. It was exactly seven weeks and a day following the Feast of Passover when the Holy Spirit descended on them during Pentecost. The disciples became human wave loaves; speaking in a variety of tongues. The Holy Spirit, as represented by the fine flour, descended upon the disciples, as redeemed sinners who typified the added yeast. As prophesized in Jeremiah 31:33-34, Ezekiel 36:26-27, and Joel 2:28-29 the Holy Spirit filled the disciples' hearts.

The Festival of Trumpets aka Rosh Hashanah

This feast was held on the first day of the seventh month. During this celebration ram's horns called shofars were blown, marking the beginning of ten days of introspection and repentance. Burnt and sin offerings were brought before the Lord. Immediately followed this festival was the Day of Atonement. Later this Feast of Trumpet became known as Rosh Hashanah or New Year's Day. It was observed by the blowing of trumpets. Read more in Leviticus 23:24-32 and Numbers 29:1-46.

CHAPTER 10

THE DAY OF ATONEMENT
AND FEAST OF TABERNACLES

In the Mosaic Covenant, God commanded the Israelites to conduct a sacred ceremony each year known as the Day of Atonement or Yom Kippur. On that day, and that day only, Aaron as High Priest was allowed to enter the Holy of Holies. The solemnity was emphasized by God telling Moses to warn Aaron that he was never to enter except on that day or he would die. It wasn't a ceremony to be taken lightly.

Inside the Tabernacle Aaron's presence represented the entire nation of Israel. Normally he wore his regal apparel, but not on this day. He still wore his specially designed turban but he robed himself in just a plain white linen tunic.

Before representing the nation on this day, Aaron's first responsibility was to deal with own sins. He was required to ceremoniously wash himself. The significance of the washing identified the need for the priest, and subsequently all mankind, to be cleansed of sin. After washing, he was required to walk over to the Brazen Altar and sacrifice a bull. The bull was a sin offering for himself. After killing the bull, Aaron was to capture the bull's blood in a basin and carry it into the Holy Place. After entering, he was to walk toward the Altar of Incense and place burning coals into a golden censer. Then, filling his hand with a specially blended type of incense known as "salted and pure and sacred," Aaron was to part the beautifully woven curtain that separated the Holy Place from the Holy of Holies. Inside the Holy of Holies was God's throne room on earth. Here God's Shekinah glory appeared as intense light. Once inside, Aaron dispensed the incense from his hand over the hot coals. The reaction diffused into a divinely fragrant white cloud. Then, seven times, Aaron was to sprinkle the bull's blood on top of the Mercy Seat. After accomplishing this task, Aaron was to turn away from God's holy presence and exit the room via the thick curtain. Returning to the outer courtyard, he had additional tasks. After seeking forgiveness for himself, he was now challenged to seek clemency for the entire nation of Israel.

In the outer court were two goats without blemish, each of whom represented the nation of Israel. The goats were brought to Aaron and lots cast to see which goat would be sacrificed, and which one's life would be spared. The sacrificial goat was taken, and in front of the people, Aaron had to cut its jugular vein. The goat's blood was poured out into a basin and accepted by God as a covering for the people's sins. Like before, Aaron was required to carry the animal's blood into the holiest part of the tabernacle. Inside the Holy of Holies Aaron was to reverently sprinkle the goat's blood on top of the Mercy Seat seven times. This was considered a Sin Offering.

God's Mercy Seat

The Mercy Seat represented God's earthly throne. It was covered in gold and fashioned with cherubim positioned at each end. Between the cherubim, just above the Mercy Seat, was God's presence appearing as an intense, penetrating, bright light. Below the Mercy Seat was the Ark of the Covenant and it, too, was covered in gold.

In review, inside the Ark of the Covenant were three items. 1) The stone tablets with the Ten Commandments written on them; 2) Aaron's rod that budded, and 3) a pot of manna miraculously preserved by God.

Just above the Ark, God looked down on the blood smeared Mercy Seat. And by God's Covenant with Adam, the animal's blood temporarily covered the sins of the Israelites, granting them mercy instead of judgment.

Scape Goat

Day of Atonement Scape Goat

After exiting the Tabernacle, Aaron again was to return to the courtyard. There he was to take the scape goat and lay his hands on its head, confessing outloud every filthy sin of the people. The goat was then escorted into the wilderness by a priest, and sent away never to return. Aaron and the people would watch as the priest led their confessed sin substitute out of sight. The people understood that the first goat had to die for their sins, and its blood sprinkled on the Mercy Seat. By the grace of God, the first goat's blood covered their sins. The second goat was God's way of telling them that their confessed sins were removed from judgment. With their past sins removed from sight, their fellowship with God was restored and it was a time to celebrate.

Christ in the Atonement

The Day of Atonement typified Jesus' finished work on the cross. As a sacrificial lamb, Jesus died for the remission of man's sins. And in this divine act of forgiveness, Jesus, as revealed by John the Baptist in John 1:29 became *"the Lamb of God who takes away the sin of the world!"*

The Sacrificed Lamb of God

As the Son of Man, Jesus asked, *"Father, if you are willing, take this cup from me; yet not my will, but yours be done."* And later, on the cross, Jesus cried out, *"My God, My God, why have you forsaken me?"* It was Jesus who became our ultimate blood sacrifice. As identified in 2nd Corinthians 5:21, God made him who had no sin to be sin for us, so that in him we might become the righteousness of God.

The Sacrificial Blood of Jesus

So great was Jesus' physical and emotional anguish on the Mount of Olives, that His sweat turned red with blood. Capillary blood vessels that fed Jesus' sweat glands ruptured through His skin. A physiological condition known as hematidrosis. John 19:1 records that before Jesus' execution Pilate had him flogged. Flogging required the use of a flagrum, a whip made out of leather straps. Intertwined with its braided leather straps were lead balls and razor sharp sheep bones. These items dangling from the whip's tip. Jesus would have been stripped of His clothes and had his hands tied to an upright post. Next, Jesus would have been beaten across his back, buttocks, and legs. The blunt force of the lead balls and sheep bones would have cut deeply into His skin and underlying skeletal muscles. The action would have resulted in quivering bands of raw, bleeding flesh. His blood loss would have been severe and the pain, excruciating. A crown of thorns was pressed down into his scalp, oozing out more blood and causing Jesus greater agony. Then Jesus was given a robe to wear. At the site of His crucifixion, Jesus' robe was removed and the coagulated wounds on his back reopened, causing them to bleed. The pain had to be unbearable. When Jesus' wrists and feet were callously nailed to the cross with large, tapered iron spikes, even more blood was shed. On the cross Jesus' stained blood was evident both horizontally and vertically. After enduring such cruelty, Jesus remarked, *"It is finished."* He bowed his head and the slain Lamb of God gave up His Spirit.

Jesus' sacrifice fulfilled the passage found in Isaiah 53:4-8. *"Surely he took up our pain and bore our suffering, yet we considered him punished by God, stricken by him, and afflicted. But he was pierced for our transgressions, he was crushed for our iniquities; the punishment that brought us peace was on him, and by his wounds we are healed. We all, like sheep, have gone astray, each of us has turned to our own way; and the LORD has laid on him the iniquity of us all. He was oppressed and afflicted, yet he did not open his mouth; He was led like a lamb to the slaughter, and as a sheep before its shearers is silent, so he did not open his mouth. By oppression and judgment he was taken away. Yet who of his generation protested? For he was cut off from the land of the living; for the transgression of my people he was punished."*

When Jesus arose from the grave, God the Father declared that mankind's sins (past, present and future) had been dealt with forever. As recorded in Matthew 27:50-53 (NIV), *"And when Jesus had cried out again in a loud voice, he gave up his spirit. At that moment the curtain of the temple was torn in two from top to bottom. The earth shook, the rocks split and the tombs broke open. The bodies of many holy people who had died were raised to life. They came out of the tombs after Jesus' resurrection and went into the holy city, appearing to many people."* Significantly, on Easter Sunday, God took man's robe, stained with transgressions, and replaced it with His white garment of righteousness. What a covenant exchange!

The Significance of Jesus' Redemptive Blood

Under the Old Covenant the people's sins were only covered, never eradicated. But now, by Jesus offering His own blood, sin was dealt its death blow.

Hebrews 9:13-14 tells us, *"The blood of goats and bulls and the ashes of a heifer sprinkled on those who are ceremonially unclean sanctify them so that they are outwardly clean. How much more, then, will the blood of Christ, who through the eternal Spirit offered himself unblemished to God, cleanse our consciences from acts that lead to death, so that we may serve the living God!"*

The example of Aaron entering the Holy of Holies, typified Christ's entrance into heaven with his own blood. And now as our High Priest, Jesus makes intercession for all believers.

Hebrews 9:11-12 further reminds us, *"But when Christ came as high priest of the good things that are now already here, he went through the greater and more perfect tabernacle that is not made with human hands, that is to say, is not a part of this creation. He did not enter by means of the blood of goats and calves; but he entered the Most Holy Place once for all by his own blood, thus obtaining eternal redemption."*

Aaron's Final Responsibility

After watching the scape goat leave the camp site, Aaron was to return to the Tabernacle and wash himself and his clothes. After washing, Aaron was allowed to put on his regal apparel, returning to announce that as a nation their sins had been covered. Then Aaron was to present a burnt offering up to God as shouts of joy were lifted up by the people. What a day!

The Feast of Tabernacle or Feast of Booths

The Feast of Tabernacle or Feast of Booths was an eight day feast which began five days after the Day of Atonement. It coincided with the end of the fall harvest. During this feast the Israelites were to dwell in booths or tabernacles constructed out of tree branches. The Israelites celebrated God's continued provision, remembering His provision and protection during their years in the wilderness. It began and ended on a Sabbath day. During the festival grain offerings were offered up to God.

SALT COVENANTS

In biblical times, blood and salt were often symbolically interchanged. Salt is an incorruptible preservative, and like blood, it, too, is necessary to sustain life. The eating of salt between men in Middle Eastern cultures is customarily a pledge of fidelity, binding a covenant of friendship. Not surprisingly, salt covenants and blood covenants are considered sacred bonds.

By eating food-containing salt (bread), covenant friends might say, "There is salt between us," or "He has eaten of my salt." In other words, eating salt together committed the parties to responsibilities for both protection and provision. Shame would be brought to anyone who ate salt with another person and then betrayed them. It would be said that they "betrayed the salt."

Old and New Testament Salt Covenants

A Salt Covenant was first mentioned as a required part of the

Hebrew peoples' grain offering. Later, in Ezekiel, a reference to was made relative to all sacrificial offerings.

- *"Season all your grain offerings with salt. Do not leave the salt of the covenant of your God out of your grain offerings; add salt to all your offerings."* Leviticus 2:13

- *"You are to offer them before the Lord, and the priests are to sprinkle salt on them and sacrifice them as a burnt offering to the Lord."* Ezekiel 43:24

Salt was used as a preservative to sanctify all altar sacrifices. The salt foreshadowed the preservation of eternal life through the ultimate "salt sacrifice" in Jesus.

A Covenant of Salt was mentioned a second time in Numbers 18:19 relative to a promise of an everlasting priesthood. *"Whatever is set aside from the holy offerings the Israelites present to the Lord I give to you and your sons and daughters as your perpetual share. It is an everlasting covenant of salt before the Lord for both you and your offspring."* And as noted in Hebrew 7:20-28, when Jesus was raised from the grave, He fulfilled this Salt Covenant by becoming our perpetual High Priest.

In this chapter, God spoke directly with Aaron, explaining his role in God's earthly priesthood. God placed Aaron directly in charge of the offerings to be presented back to God. Salt was a perpetual reminder of the covenant. And probably because salt kept meat from spoiling, it became emblematic of purity. *"And it was not without an oath! Others became priests without any oath, but he became a priest with an oath when God said to him: "The Lord has sworn and will not change his mind: You are a priest forever. Because of this oath, Jesus has become the guarantor of a better covenant. Now there have been many of those priests, since death prevented them from continuing in office; but because Jesus lives forever, he has a permanent priesthood. Therefore he is able to save completely those who come to God through him, because he always lives to intercede for them. Such a high priest truly meets our need—one who is holy, blameless, pure, set apart from sinners, exalted above the heavens. Unlike the other high priests, he does not need to offer sacrifices day after day, first for his own sins, and then for the sins of the people. He sacrificed for their sins once for all when he offered himself. For the law appoints as high priests men in all their weakness; but the oath, which came after the law, appointed the Son, who has been made perfect forever."*

A final covenant of salt was mentioned in 2 Chronicles 13:5 when the kingdom of Israel was given over to King David. *"Don't you know that the Lord, the God of Israel, has given the kingship of Israel to David and his descendants forever by a covenant of salt?"*

Again, in Luke 1:32-33 we read about the fulfillment of this salt promise in Jesus. *"He will be great and will be called the Son of the Most High. The Lord God will give him the throne of his father David, and he will reign over Jacob's descendants forever; his kingdom will never end."*

Salt of the Earth

Sitting down at the kitchen table with fresh, ripe tomatoes from the garden and a salt shaker is a chance to enjoy a slice of heaven. The salt enhances the flavor. Jesus said in Matthew 5:13-14, "*You are the salt of the earth. But if the salt loses its saltiness, how can it be made salty again? It is no longer good for anything, except to be thrown out and trampled underfoot.*"

Pure salt makes people thirsty. By being "the salt of the earth" others should thirst for what God's people have. The Apostle Peter has identified God's people as a "***chosen generation and a royal priesthood.***" By living out this high calling, God's people purify and flavor those around them. As believers, don't ever "betray the salt."

The Shabbat

As noted previously, just before the bread is broken into smaller pieces and passed to family members, salt is sprinkled over the entire loaf. The Shabbat memorializes the "salt covenant." In one respect, the family's table becomes a makeshift altar. The covenant meal concludes the following evening with a special blessing called the Havdalah, recited over a cup of wine.

CHAPTER 12

JOSHUA AND THE PROMISE LAND

The Palestinian Covenant

As described in Deuteronomy, Chapters 29 and 30, just before Moses died, God made another covenant promise referred to as the Palestinian or Land Covenant. The covenant was made in Moab while the Israelites were waiting to enter the Promised Land. Before making this covenant, God reminded Moses that Israel would be blessed abundantly if they obeyed the Mosaic Law, and cursed if they disobeyed. Then God gave Moses an unconditional, eternal covenant.

God told Moses, *"When the people finally learn to trust me and keep my commandments I will have compassion on them. And I will gather them from all of the nations where they have been scattered, back to the land of their ancestors. I will circumcise their hearts so that they will love Me with their whole heart and soul. I will judge their enemies and they will be obedient."*

Notice how this covenant focuses on a future time when God returns Israel to the land promised as outlined in Genesis 15:18-21. Unlike the conditional promises of the Mosaic Covenant, the Palestinian Covenant was not dependent upon Israel's obedience. Instead, it is an unconditional covenant. A promise that one day will manifest itself in reality.

Leadership Transition to Joshua

The generation of Israelites who came out of bondage in Egypt were complainers. God provided them with His protection, and manna to eat, but they moaned for something more than God's daily provision. Out of compassion, God directed droves of quail into their encampment. One time, while the people were encamped near Rephidim, there was no water for them or their livestock to drink, and they complained to Moses. Moses was worn out with their incessant whining and prayed to God for help. God told Moses to take the same rod used to part the Red Sea and strike a particular rock at Horeb. Moses did as was instructed and the Lord produced water for the people and their herds to drink.

Later, in Numbers, Chapter 20, we find that the people came to an area near Kadesh, and again there wasn't any water to drink. The people protested and contended with Moses and his brother Aaron. Before the Lord, Moses and Aaron fell on their faces asking for help. God told Moses to take the same rod and gather the people. He was to SPEAK to the rock and then out of the rock would flow running water. So Moses gathered the people. But instead of following God's instructions, Moses' anger got the best of him. Moses called the people rebels and said, "*Must WE bring water for you out of this rock?*" Then angrily, Moses STRUCK the rock twice and water gushed out. By striking the rock instead of speaking to the rock, Moses disobeyed God's instructions. And God responded, "*Because you did not trust in me enough to honor me as holy in the sight of the Israelites, you will not bring this community into the land I give them.*"

At first blush, God's chastisement seemed severe. But looking at it from God's perspective the punishment was appropriate. Out of anger and frustration, Moses rejected God's command to speak to the rock, and instead took complete control himself. He called the people rebels. Yet by his actions, Moses was the one rebelling against God. In direct disobedience to God's command, Moses struck the rock, not once, but twice. On a spiritual level, Jesus is the Rock of our salvation and out of Him comes living water. By striking the rock, Moses was metaphorically striking Christ, who was offering water to the people. (See I Corinthians 10:4). By not speaking to the rock, Moses was usurping God's place in the miracle. And by his saying "we," Moses was technically taking some of the credit for the miracle. Obviously, taking matters into his own hands was a devastating mistake. "*Because you did not trust in me enough to honor me as holy in the sight of the Israelites, you will not bring this community into the land I give them.*" And true to His word, God did not allow Moses or Aaron to enter the Promised Land. Regardless of God's punishment, God loved Moses. We know this because on the Mount of Transfiguration the disciples saw with Jesus, Elijah and who else, God's dear friend, Moses.

The Bronze Serpent

The Bronze Serpent

As covenant people, the Israelites failed miserably to honor and trust in God. In the 21st chapter of Numbers we read where the people continued to rebel against God and His provision for them. Out of righteous judgment for breaking covenant, God sent fiery serpents to live among them. Their sting was fatal and many of the people died. Recognizing their sin, the people came to Moses and asked him to intercede on their behalf. They wanted desperately to be released from God's judgment. Moses prayed and God told him, *"Make a bronze serpent and put it up on a pole; anyone who is bitten can look at it and live."* So Moses made it and put it up on a pole. And any Israelite bitten by a serpent who gazed upon the serpent, lived. If a person wanted to be saved they had to look upon the serpent who represented their rebellious, sinful nature.

The required exercise was an analogous shadow of Christ who became our substance in the New Covenant. Jesus testified in John 3:14-15. *"Just as Moses lifted up the snake in the wilderness, so the Son of Man must be lifted up, that everyone who believes may have eternal life in him.*" The bronze serpent on the pole was analogous of the people's sin, and the "up lifted" pole typified the cross at Calvary. And like all of the Israelites who looked up and lived, all sinners who look up to the cross and believe shall live forever with Christ.

Joshua and Caleb

A couple of years into the Israelites wilderness journey, the Lord told Moses to send twelve men (one from each tribe) into Canaan. It was to be a 40-day mission to explore the land and its inhabitants. When the twelve men returned, ten of them gave Moses and the people fearful reports. They reported that giants lived in the land and that their cities were well fortified and impossible to defeat. In abhorrence, God listened to their negative reports, witnessing their lack of faith in Him and His awesome power. Equally disgusting, the people listening bought into the same fears and lack of faith. The people remarked to one another, "We should choose a leader and go back to Egypt." But two of the men, Joshua and Caleb, gave different reports.

Joshua and Caleb fully believed God would go ahead of them and conquer every enemy. To them it was a land of milk and honey, and as God's emissaries, they eagerly wanted to conquer the land. Joshua stood up and told the assembly that the land was exceedingly good, and that the Lord would lead and give it to them. He told the assembly, *"Only don't rebel against the Lord. And don't be afraid of people of the land because we will devour them."* When he finished speaking, the faithless people talked about stoning him. Moses pleaded with God to pardon the people's insolence. God acknowledged Moses' intercessory plea, but their rebellious nature had consequences. The faithless people would have to spend 40 years wandering in the Sinai desert, one year for each day of disbelief.

Consequences

In Numbers, Chapter 14, the Lord said to Moses, *"I have forgiven them, as you asked. Nevertheless, as surely as I live and as surely as the glory of the LORD fills the whole earth, not one of those who saw my glory and the signs I performed in Egypt and in the wilderness but who disobeyed me and tested me ten times not one of them will ever see the land I promised on oath to their ancestors. No one who has treated me with contempt will ever see it. But because my servant Caleb has a different spirit and follows me wholeheartedly, I will bring him into the land he went to, and his descendants will inherit it.*

"How long will this wicked community grumble against me? I have heard the complaints of these grumbling Israelites. So tell them, 'As surely as I live, declares the LORD, I will do to you the very thing I heard you say: In this wilderness your bodies will fall, every one of you twenty years old or more who was counted in the census and who has grumbled against me. Not one of you will enter the land I swore with uplifted hand to make your home, except Caleb and Joshua. As for your children that you said would be taken as plunder, I will bring them in to enjoy the land you

have rejected. But as for you, your bodies will fall in this wilderness. Your children will be shepherds here for forty years, suffering for your unfaithfulness, until the last of your bodies lies in the wilderness.

"For forty years—one year for each of the forty days you explored the land—you will suffer for your sins and know what it is like to have me against you." I, the Lord, have spoken, and I will surely do these things to this whole wicked community, which has banded together against me. They will meet their end in this wilderness; here they will die." So the men Moses had sent to explore the land, who returned and made the whole community grumble against him by spreading a bad report about it, these men who were responsible for spreading the bad report about the land were struck down and died of a plague before the LORD. Of the men who went to explore the land, only Joshua son of Nun and Caleb survived."

God's Covenant Promise to Joshua

After 40 years of wandering in the wilderness, the covenant torch passed from Moses to his protégé, Joshua. Joshua was a descendent of Joseph and was chosen by God to physically conquer the Promised Land. He was born and raised in the land of Goshen. Joshua witnessed God's judgment on the Egyptians (all the signs and wonders); the parting of the Red Sea; the provision of manna and quail in the Negev desert; God's awesome presence on Mt. Sinai; and how God empowered Moses to lead His people.

After the death of Moses the Lord said to Joshua (Joshua 1:1-11), "*Moses my servant is dead. Now then, you and all these people, get ready to cross the Jordan River into the land I am about to give to them—to the Israelites. I will give you every place where you set your foot, as I promised Moses. Your territory will extend from the desert to Lebanon, and from the great river, the Euphrates—all the Hittite country—to the Mediterranean Sea in the west. No one will be able to stand against you all the days of your life. As I was with Moses, so I will be with you; I will never leave you nor forsake you. Be strong and courageous, because you will lead these people to inherit the land I swore to their ancestors to give them.*

"*Be strong and very courageous. Be careful to obey all the law my servant Moses gave you; do not turn from it to the right or to the left, that you may be successful wherever you go. Keep this Book of the Law always on your lips; meditate on it day and night, so that you may be careful to do everything written in it. Then you will be prosperous and successful. Have I not commanded you? Be strong and courageous. Do not be afraid; do not be discouraged, for the LORD your God will be with you wherever you go.*" *So Joshua ordered the officers of the people: "Go through the camp and tell the people, 'Get your provisions ready. Three days from now you will cross the Jordan here to go in and take possession of the land the LORD your God is giving you for your own.'*"

Comparison: Joshua and Jesus

- Joshua obeyed God's command to go and conquer the land for His chosen people. Jesus obeyed His Father's

126

command to conquer death, securing eternity for all of His people.

- Joshua came to establish a kingdom on earth while Jesus came to establish a kingdom yet to come.

- Joshua sent conquering soldiers into a spiritually dark land while Jesus sent His disciples out into a spiritually dark world.

Rahab the Harlot

Before Joshua entered the Promised Land, he sent spies to scout out the terrain and the town of Jericho. Jericho's inhabitants were afraid of Joshua. After the town's men became apprised that the spies were in the city, they sought after them. A harlot named Rahab gave Joshua's spies protective cover. She hid them under stalks of flax on her roof. When the men of Jericho came inquiring about the spies' whereabouts, Rahab lied to them. She told the men that they had been there but left. Interestingly, Rahab heard the same news that put fear in the hearts of everyone else in Jericho, but instead of fear, her heart was filled with faith. Rahab's faith led her to speak to the spies. In Joshua 2:12-13 she said, *"Now then, please swear to me by the Lord that you will show kindness to my family, because I have shown kindness to you. Give me a sure sign that you will spare the lives of my father and mother, my brothers and sisters, and all who belong to them—and that you will save us from death."*

In return for protecting Joshua's spies, she was instructed by God's servants to drop a scarlet cord from her window. Further, they told her in Joshua 2:12-13, "*Unless, when we enter the land, you have tied this scarlet cord in the window through which you let us down, and unless you have brought your father and mother, your brothers and all your family into your house. If any of them go outside your house into the street, their blood will be on their own heads; we will not be responsible. As for those who are in the house with you, their blood will be on our head if a hand is laid on them.*" Rahab did as instructed, and when Jericho fell she and her household was saved.

Joshua Reinstates Circumcision

During their days in the wilderness, God's command to circumcise every male child was ignored. To restore the covenant God had made with Abraham, the Lord told Joshua "*Make flint knives and circumcise the Israelites again.*" "*So Joshua made flint knives and circumcised the Israelites. Now this is why he did so: All those who came out of Egypt—all the men of military age—died in the wilderness on the way after leaving Egypt. All the people that came out had been circumcised, but all the people born in the wilderness during the journey from Egypt had not. The Israelites had moved about in the wilderness forty years until all the men who were of military age when they left Egypt had died, since they had not obeyed the Lord. For the Lord had sworn to them that they would not see the land he had solemnly promised their ancestors to give us, a land flowing with milk and honey. So he raised up their sons in their place, and these were the ones Joshua circumcised. They were still uncircumcised because they had not been circumcised on the way. And after the whole nation had been circumcised, they remained where they were in camp until they were healed. Then the Lord said to Joshua, 'Today I have rolled away the reproach of Egypt from you.'* " Joshua 5:2-9

With the circumcision task completed, the Israelites celebrated a Passover meal. Now the Israelites, under Joshua's leadership, were prepared to conquer the Promised Land. Their circumcision revitalized the nation's blood covenant with God.

Battle of Jericho

When nearing Jericho, Joshua looked up and saw a man standing with a drawn sword. Joshua approached and ask if he was friend or foe. The man remarked, "Neither." He identified himself as Commander of God's army, sent to take personal charge of the ensuing battle. Joshua fell facedown and paid homage to the man. The man told Joshua to remove his sandals because he was standing on holy ground. The person Joshua encountered was the pre-incarnate Son of Man. Who else had the right to declare the place he stood as holy? The Battle of Jericho was going to be the Lord's battle. Victory was assured! It would be taken by faith, not force.

Joshua was told to march with his men around the city and at an appointed time, the priests were to blow their trumpets. God's invisible army would break down Jericho's fortified wall. All Joshua and his men had to do was watch in awe. When Jericho's wall fell, Rahab faithfully did as she was instructed. She dropped the scarlet cord from her window. The chord was symbolic of protective blood. So while death and destruction befell the city of Jericho, Rahab and her family remained safe. Interestingly, in Bible history, Rahab married an Israelite named Salmon, and she became the great-great-grandmother of King David. Rahab is mentioned, too, as being a distant relative of Joseph, Jesus' step-father. God works in mysterious ways.

Covenant Oath with the Gibeonites

Joshua's command by God was to conquer Canaan and divide the land among the descendants of Jacob's twelve sons. Under God's orders as outlined in Deuteronomy 7:1-2, Joshua's band of soldiers were to invade and crush the pagan people living in the land. A neighboring city called Gibeon heard about Joshua's conquests and were justifiably afraid. They knew he was a fearless man of God, and to prevent their annihilation, the Gibeonites tricked the Israelites into making a peaceful covenant with them.

Gibeon was located about seven miles northwest of Jerusalem and less than 15 miles from where Joshua was encamped at Gilgal. Cunningly, a small band of Gibeonites dressed themselves as men from a far country. They showed Joshua's men stale bread and dry wineskins as evidence of the faked journey. Then they asked the Israelites to enter into a peaceful covenant with them. Foolishly, without vigilant, prayerful consideration, the gullible Israelites entered into a covenant.

Joshua 9:15 tells us, *"Then Joshua made a treaty of peace with them (Gibeon) to let them live, and the leaders of the assembly rati-fied it by oath."* Afterwards, the Israeli leadership discovered their trickery, but it was too late. Israel was in covenant with God, and the Gibeonites, now in covenant with Joshua, became legitimate part-ners with Israel's God. That's how covenant works. As strange as it sounds, even based on a lie, the Gibeonites became benefactors of a sacred, unbreakable covenant. The Israelites became bound by their covenant promise. The lesson is clear. Christians must be wary of seduction because it is to be feared as much as combat.

Shortly after the deceptive covenant was made, the people of Gibeon found themselves under attack by a coalition of five jealous and fuming kings. As their covenant partner, Joshua's army was obligated to honor the covenant and come to their rescue. So Joshua's army prevailed over the five kings and saved their cov-enant partner from destruction.

Joshua Conquers Canaan

When Joshua and his men conquered the land, all pagan and evil influences were to be destroyed. God commanded Joshua to conquer and wipe out every kingdom he encountered. God com-manded the conquered cities to be destroyed because the pagan people in Canaan chose to worship idols, to engage in temple pros-titution, homosexuality, orgies, snake worship, and even infant sacrifice. In order for the Israelites to start over, the annihilation of these practices was necessary. Under God's command, Joshua defeated 31 kings. The victories were a living testament to God's awesome power and Israel's claim to the Promised Land.

After Joshua's days of conquering were over, he assigned conquered territory to the various tribes. Joshua told the tribal leaders that their job wasn't over, more Canaanite villages needed eradicating and, if left untouched, the enemy would slowly rebuild and become a thorn in their future. With the exception of the priestly tribe of Levi, each of the twelve tribes was appointed land as an inheritance. Joshua's warning, though, went unheeded and the tribes failed to continue their assignments. Instead they made alliances with heathen nations and their disobedience brought about fighting that continues to this very day.

Choose this day!

After dividing the conquered land, Joshua gave a final sermon. His words from that sermon still echo loudly today. *"Choose for yourselves this day whom you will serve, as for me and my house, we will serve the Lord."* Joshua 24:15

CHAPTER 13

THE DAVIDIC COVENANT

Anointing a King

Biographical accounts of a shepherd boy named David are found in I and II Samuel. David was chosen by God and anointed by the prophet Samuel to become the second King of Israel. And with God's favor, David led an extraordinary life.

A prophet named Samuel was summoned by God to go to David's father's house in Bethlehem. His assignment was to anoint a future king. This anointed one would one day replace the current King (Saul) with whom God was displeased. Samuel arrived and asked to visit with the father of the household, a man named Jesse. Samuel asked to speak with his sons in order to determine which one God had chosen to become Israel's future king. The first son that Samuel looked upon was the eldest son, Eliab. By all outward appearances, Samuel thought he might be the one. But God revealed to Samuel that he was not to consider his appearance or height, because God was interested in a man's heart, not his external appearance. So Eliab was rejected. Samuel knew then, that when the right son appeared, God's Spirit would move inside him.

Jesse called his next oldest son, Abinadab, and had him pass in front of Samuel. And the Lord rejected him, too. Next Shammah passed in front of Jesse, and he was not chosen either. In total, Jesse had seven of his sons pass in front of Samuel, none of whom passed God's test. Samuel asked Jesse, "Are these all your sons?" Jesse told him that the youngest was out in the fields tending the family's sheep. Samuel asked that he be sent for, and he would wait. When David arrived, Samuel saw that he was a handsome lad with all the appearance of glowing health. Then the Lord told Samuel, "*Anoint him because he is the one.*" So Samuel anointed David and from that day forth the Spirit of the Lord came powerfully upon him.

Remarkably, while David was in the fields tending his father's sheep, God's eyes were watching him from above. Though David was out of sight, he certainly wasn't forgotten or dismissed by God. And neither are you! While waiting on God's timing for his kingly appointment, David was called upon to serve.

King Saul had displeased God and at times exhibited a troubled soul. Music seemed to ease his anxious spirit. One of King Saul's servants told him about David's ability to play the lyre. The servant remarked, too, that David was brave, and a warrior, and most importantly, God was with him. Having heard of his abilities, King Saul asked David to play the lyre. After playing, David would return to tending his father's flock.

David and Goliath

At this time Israel was engaged in a battle with the Philistines. The Philistines had marched toward the heart of Judah where Saul's army had blocked their advance. Saul's army set up headquarters near a valley sandwiched between two giant cliffs. The Philistines positioned themselves on the opposite side of this valley floor knows as the Valley of Elah.

David's three older brothers were recruiting into the Israeli army and serving close to the front lines. Jesse, David's father, sent David to the battlegrounds to check on his brothers' well-being. David took provisions of roasted grain, chunks of cheese, and several loaves of bread. After arriving at the encampment, David overheard Goliath defying the armies of the living God. Then he listened carefully to the reward for any man killing the giant and removing the reproach from Israel. So David decided to be the man. But when he stepped up to the plate, his oldest brother became angry with him. It probably stung having his youngest brother receive the anointing and it made him jealous. But instead of challenging his older brother, David ignored his insults and just walked away.

The Philistine giant's name was Goliath. Appearing fully outfitted in armor and standing 9'9" Goliath was intimidating. Every day for the last 40 days he had offered a challenge. Goliath would represent all of the Philistines, while his opponent would represent the entire nation of Israel. The issue of victory and national supremacy was to be settled in those two individuals. Whoever won the battle, their country would be considered the victor.

Incensed by the giant's arrogance, and led by the Holy Spirit, David offered to fight Goliath. King Saul heard about David's desire to fight Goliath and summoned him. Saul questioned David's ability to fight this warrior giant, meeting David's faith with his disbelief. But David responded by telling Saul that the same Lord who rescued him from the paws of a lion and a bear, would rescue him from the hand of this uncircumcised Philistine. David had faith in God and was unafraid.

Saul dressed David in armor but David took it all off. Instead, he chose five smooth stones from a nearby stream. In his own flesh, David was just as powerless against Goliath as everyone else. And judging by David's appearance, he was no champion. But filled with the Holy Spirit, David had confidence in God's power. He had stood up, spoke out, and was ready to stand his ground.

Due to David's short stature, Goliath insulted him, and then cursed David. But when Goliath cursed David, he was also cursing God. And that was something God wouldn't allow to go unpunished. David responded to Goliath's words with conviction, "*You come against me with sword and spear and javelin, but I come against you in the name of the Lord Almighty, the God of the armies of Israel, whom you have defiled. This day the Lord will deliver you into my hands, and I'll strike you down and cut off your head... And the whole world will know that there is a God in*

Israel. All those gathered here will know that it is not by sword or spear that the Lord saves; for the battle is the Lord's, and he will give all of you into our hands."

Using a slingshot, David heaved one of his gathered stones at Goliath striking him in the forehead. The giant was stunned and fell to the ground. Then David took Goliath's own sword and beheaded him. Afterwards, he brought Goliath's head to Jerusalem. The head would be a warning to the Jebusites, who were inhabitants of Jerusalem, not to mess with God's people. That day, David's victory rescued the nation of Israel from the hands of the Philistines. Similarly, Jesus' victory over death at Calvary became a triumph for all believers.

David's Life after Goliath

For defeating Goliath, David was offered one of King Saul's daughters in marriage. But David humbly refused. He wasn't accustomed to palace living and felt more comfortable with his shepherd lifestyle. King Saul's son, Prince Jonathan, was enchanted with David. So much so that Jonathan initiated a very one-sided covenant exchange with David.

Jonathan took off the princely robe he was wearing and gave it to David, along with his tunic, his sword, his bow, and belt. In exchange, David had nothing to offer. Symbolically, Jonathan, heir to the throne, was subordinating his position and committing all of his strength and ability to fight to David. Their covenant made it perfectly clear that if anyone harmed David, they were attacking the Prince. And that the Prince would defend David, even if it meant losing his own life. And his was an everlasting covenant that could not be broken. Jonathan's action greatly displeased his father. It wasn't fitting behavior for a member of the royal family to submit authority to anyone. But Jonathan did.

The Great One-Sided Exchange

Jonathan's action were illustrative of the Great One-Sided Exchange found in the Covenant of Redemption. By covenant, God joined sinful man to Himself by making Jesus mankind's bearer of sin and substitutionary sacrifice. In order for God to declare mankind righteous before Him, Jesus had to pay the death penalty for mankind's sins. This unselfish act of God's love, mercy and grace, imputed the perfect righteousness of Jesus on His followers. It was an incredible exchange. The Son of God exchanged His robe of perfect, righteous standing before the Father, for a filthy robe laden with sins, sickness, sorrows and guilt.

Philippians 2:6-11 reminds us of this incredible exchange. *"Who (God the Son), being in the very nature God, did not consider equality with God something to be used to his own advantage; rather, he made himself nothing by taking the very nature of a servant, being made in human likeness. And being found in appearance as a man, he humbled himself by becoming obedient to death-even death on a cross! Therefore God exalted him to the highest place and gave him the name that is above every name, that at the name of Jesus every knee should bow, in heaven and on earth and under the earth, and every tongue acknowledge that Jesus Christ is Lord, to the glory of God the Father."* By confessing Jesus as Lord, Christians join in the Son's covenant with the Father. And symbolically, Christians are given a robe of righteousness (Isaiah 61:10) in exchange for *"filthy rags"* ravaged by sin (Isaiah 64:6).

Covenant Promises

Eventually David married a different daughter of Saul's named Michal. She loved David. The couple ate at the king's table with Michal's brother, Jonathan. King Saul, became insanely jealous of David and on several occasions sought to kill him. Fearing for his life, David fled. While on the run, Jonathan caught up with him. David said to Jonathan, *"As for you, show kindness to your servant, for you have brought me into a covenant with you before the Lord. If I am guilty, then kill me yourself! Why hand me over to your father?"* Jonathan remarked to David, *"But show me unfailing kindness like the Lord's kindness as long as I live, so that I may not be killed, and do not ever cut off your kindness from my family—not even when the Lord has cut off every one of David's enemies from the face of the earth."* Jonathan had David reaffirm his oath, because he loved him as he did himself. Then Jonathan said to David, *"Go in peace, for we have sworn friendship with each other in the name of the Lord, saying, 'The Lord is witness between you and me, and between your descendants and my descendants forever.' "*

Later, we read in 1 Samuel 23: 15-18 that while David was in the Desert of Ziph, he learned that Saul had come out to take his life. Jonathan went to David and said, *"Don't be afraid. My father Saul will not lay a hand on you. You will be king over Israel, and I will be second to you. Even my father Saul knows this."* The two men talked and made a vow before the Lord. In this passage of scripture, Jonathan clearly subordinated his princely position as rightful heir to the throne.

Then around 1010 B.C., King Saul and Prince Jonathan were engaged in a battle and both men died on the battlefield. David was announced as Israel's new King, and God entered into a covenant with David. The covenant guaranteed the throne of David forever (2 Samuel 7:16), establishing his seed as the eventual King of Kings (Isaiah 9:6-7).

The Davidic Covenant

In II Samuel 7:8-16, the prophet Nathan appeared in front of King David and told him, *"This is what the Lord Almighty says: I took you from the pasture, from tending the flock, and appointed you ruler over my people Israel. I have been with you wherever you have gone, and I have cut off all your enemies from before you. Now I will make your name great, like the names of the greatest men on earth. And I will provide a place for my people Israel and will plant them so that they can have a home of their own and no longer be disturbed. Wicked people will not oppress them anymore, as they did at the beginning and have done ever since the time I appointed leaders over my people Israel. I will also give you rest from all your enemies. The Lord declares to you that the Lord himself will establish a house for you: When your days are over and you rest with your ancestors, I will raise up your offspring to succeed you, your own flesh and blood, and I will establish his kingdom. He is the one who will build a house for my Name, and I will establish the throne of his kingdom forever. I will be his father, and he will be my son. When he does wrong, I will punish him with a rod wielded by men, with floggings inflicted by human hands. But my love will never be taken away from him, as I took it away from Saul, whom I removed from before you. Your house and your kingdom will endure forever before me; your throne will be established forever.*" These prophetic words referred to David's son, Solomon, and to David's greater Son, the Messiah.

To fulfill this prophecy, Jesus had to become the seed of David. Matthew 1:1-16 traces the royal lineage of Joseph, Jesus' father by adoption, back to King David and subsequently to Abraham. The significance of this passage established Joseph as a distant heir to David's throne. Luke 1:32 describes Mary as a descendent of Judah and of the lineage of David. Therefore, as prophesied, David's "seed" manifested itself in the Son of Man. And interestingly, just as David was from Bethlehem, so the promised Messiah would be born there in a stable.

Uniquely, God's unilateral covenant promises required nothing from David. They were unconditional. God's covenant promised that David's seed would one day rule over Israel gave reference to an eternal kingdom. And that a descendant of his would one day bring peace and justice to God's people referred to Jesus's Second

Coming. On that day Israel would have a king known as "the Lord's anointed." And his kingdom would know no end. God's promise that David's seed would become ruler over Israel in His everlasting kingdom was an incredible honor.

The Apostle Paul added revelation to this prophecy when he spoke of Jesus in Acts 13:36-37, "*Now when David had served God's purpose in his own generation, he fell asleep; he was buried with his ancestors and his body decayed. But the one whom God raised from the dead did not see decay.*" The last part of the passage referred to Christ's resurrection, the one who reigns eternally.

Covenant's Continuing Adherence

David remembered his promise to Jonathan and went looking for Jonathan's heirs. David desired to bless Jonathan's children with kindness. David was informed that Jonathan had a son, who was lame on his feet, named Mephibosheth. He was hiding out in Lo Debar. Mephibosheth didn't realize that through his father, he was in covenant with the King of Israel. Because he wasn't aware of the covenant, Mephibosheth never realized his favored position.

So, too, the Covenant of Redemption between God the Father and His Son, Jesus. Though unfathomable by sinners deserving of God's judgment, this incredible, unbreakable, blood covenant makes all believers benefactors of God's divine love and amazing grace through Jesus Christ.

Once King David learned about Mephibosheth, he gave orders to bring him to the palace. When summoned to meet the king he was probably scared to death. Direct heirs like Mephibosheth would normally have been perceived as a threat to the throne and murdered. But when he arrived, King David said to him, *"Don't be afraid. I intend to show kindness to you because of my promise to your father, Jonathan. I will give you all the property that once belonged to your grandfather, King Saul, and you shall eat at the king's table!"*

Based solely on the merits of covenant, David accepted Mephibosheth as he would have Jonathan. That was enough, there wasn't any need for a further covenant. Without doing anything to deserve David's mercy, Mephibosheth was more or less adopted as a son. What saved Mephibosheth was David's blood covenant with Jonathan. So too the Covenant of Redemption between God the Father and His Son, Jesus. Though unfathomable by those spiritually lame and not deserving to eat at the King's table; this incredible, unbreakable, blood covenant, makes them benefactors of God's divine love and amazing grace. And like King David, a Christian's charge is to seek out the Mephibosheth's of this world. Telling them that because of the blood covenant between the Father and His Son, God's grace and forgiveness has been extended to them. No longer do they need to live in fear of divine judgment.

Covenant Breach

David's covenant promises made to Jonathan materialized

a second time; and once again, Mephibosheth's life was spared. During earlier fighting, when King Saul was still alive, some of his soldiers attacked and killed many of the Gibeonites. And that was wrong. The Gibeonites were protected by a covenant established with Joshua. Killing them was a serious breach to the agreed covenant. To appease the Gibeonites, King David was asked to surrender seven of King Saul's relatives. The seven men would face the same fate as the deceased Gibeonites, *"an eye for an eye."* Mephibosheth was a grandson of the late King Saul and could have been turned over to them, but for Jonathan's sake, King David protected him.

The Gibeonites came to King David and said, *"As for the man (King Saul) who destroyed us and plotted against us so that we have been decimated and have no place anywhere in Israel, let seven of his male descendants (King Saul) be given to us, to be killed, and their bodies exposed before the Lord at Gibeah of Saul—the Lord's chosen one."* So King David said, *"I will give them to you."* David *"took Armoni and Mephibosheth* (a different one), *the two sons of Aiah's daughter Rizpah, whom she had borne to Saul, together with the five sons of Saul's daughter Merab, whom she had borne to Adriel son of Barzillai the Meholathite. He handed them over to the Gibeonites who killed them and exposed their bodies on a hill before the Lord. All seven of them fell together; they were put to death during the first days of the harvest, just as the barley harvest was beginning."* Covenant adherence is never to be taken lightly.

CHAPTER 14

THE PALESTINIAN COVENANT

References to Israel's covenant land are found throughout the Bible. Included in this chapter are verses from Genesis, Deuteronomy, Ezekiel and Amos. From the Deuteronomy passage, God promised Moses that one day all of repentant Israel would reside in a Promised Land.

The Promised Land

In the book of Genesis, two covenant references are made to the land promised Abraham and his descendants. The first reference is found in Genesis 15:18. "*Unto thy seed have I given this land, from the river of Egypt* (the Nile) *unto the river Euphrates.*"

This Old Testament promise has yet to be fulfilled, but will take place during Jesus' Second Advent. At that time, all of Abraham's innumerable heirs (Jews and Gentiles) will be gathered to rule and reign with Christ.

A second reference is found in Genesis 17:4-8. *"Behold, my covenant is with you, and you shall be the father of a multitude of nations. No longer shall your name be called Abram, but your name shall be Abraham, for I have made you the father of a multitude of nations. I will make you exceedingly fruitful, and I will make you into nations, and kings shall come from you. And I will establish my covenant between me and you and your offspring after you throughout their generations for an everlasting covenant, to be God to you and to your offspring after you. And I will give to you and to your offspring after you the land of your sojourning, all the land of Canaan, for an everlasting possession, and I will be their God."*

This same promise was reiterated to Isaac, Jacob, and David.

The Palestinian Covenant

A third reference is described in Deuteronomy, Chapters 29 and 30, referred to as the Palestinian Covenant. God made this covenant promise to Moses in Moab just before Moses died. Before making His covenant promise, God reminded Moses that Israel would be blessed abundantly if they obeyed the Mosaic Law, and cursed mightily if they were disobedient. Then God gave Moses the Palestinian, unconditional, eternal covenant. God told Moses that when the people finally learned to trust and keep His commandments, He would have compassion on them. And that He would gather them from all of the nations where they had been scattered, back to the land of their ancestors. He said further that He would circumcise their hearts so that they would love Him with their whole hearts and souls. This covenant focused on a future time when Jesus returns and acquires the land promised as outlined in Genesis 15:18-21. Unlike the conditional promises of the Mosaic Covenant, the Palestinian Covenant is not dependent upon Israel's obedience. Instead, it is an unconditional, eternal covenant.

A fourth promise is found in Amos 9:14-15. "*I will bring back the captives of my people Israel; they shall build the waste cities and inhabit them. They shall plant vineyards and drink wine from them; they shall also make gardens and eat fruit from them. I will plant them in their land, and no longer shall they be pulled up from the land I have given them.*" In this ancient promise, Jesus reigns supreme, and His gathering place is of significance.

In Acts 1:9-12 Jesus ascended to heaven on the east side of Jerusalem, and according to Zechariah 14:4, this is where Jesus is expected to return. At that time, according to the prophets Zechariah and Joel, a devastating final battle will ensue around Jerusalem. Gathered nations will converge in the Valley of Jehoshaphat, aka, the Kidron Valley. It is a valley that lies between Jerusalem's Temple Mount and the Mount of Olives. Prophetically, Israel will be re-gathered, and God will judge those nations who sought to control the covenant land promised to Israel.

The Covenant Nation of Israel

Throughout Israel's checkered past, the Jewish people have

been uprooted and scattered throughout the world. But as prophesied, during Christ's Second Advent, the Israeli nation will be gathered together, and finally, peace will come to the Middle East.

In Ezekiel 34:11-16 the prophet reveals, *"For this is what the Sovereign Lord says: I myself will search for my sheep and look after them. As a shepherd looks after his scattered flock when he is with them, so will I look after my sheep. I will rescue them from all the places where they were scattered on a day of clouds and darkness. I will bring them out from the nations and gather them from the countries, and I will bring them into their own land. I will pasture them on the mountains of Israel, in the ravines and in all the settlements in the land. I will tend them in a good pasture, and the mountain heights of Israel will be their grazing land. There they will lie down in good grazing land, and there they will feed in a rich pasture on the mountains of Israel. I myself will tend my sheep and have them lie down, declares the Sovereign LORD. I will search for the lost and bring back the strays. I will bind up the injured and strengthen the weak, but the sleek and the strong I will destroy. I will shepherd the flock with justice."*

Foreshadowing Events

During World War II, the anti-Semitic Adolf Hitler believed that the Jews threatened Germany's Aryan purity. Hitler's horrific death camps exterminated an estimated six million Jewish citizens. After the war ended, England looked on the Jewish people with a sympathetic eye. And incredibly, if not miraculously, the United Nations accepted their proposal to create a Jewish state.

During World War I, a Jewish Zionist and chemist named Chaim Weizmann lent his talents to aid the English. In return for his work, Weizmann sought England's future support of a Zionist state. He began his efforts by drafting a proposal for a Jewish homeland in Palestine. Coincidentally, for political reasons, his proposal advanced England's cause. So British Foreign Secretary, Lord Arthur James Balfour, sent a letter to Lord Rothschild expressing British support for a Jewish "national home" in Palestine. It was named the Balfour Declaration and became the catalyst for an eventual Israeli state.

These are the actual words used by Arthur Balford in his letter dated November 2, 1917:

Dear Lord Rothschild,

I have much pleasure in conveying to you, on behalf of His Majesty's Government, the following declaration of sympathy with Jewish Zionist aspirations which has been submitted to, and approved by, the Cabinet.

"His Majesty's Government view with favor the establishment in Palestine of a national home for the Jewish people, and will use their best endeavors to facilitate the achievement of this object, it being clearly understood that nothing shall be done which may prejudice the civil and religious rights of existing non-Jewish communities in Palestine, or the rights and political status enjoyed by Jews in any other country."

I should be grateful if you would bring this declaration to the knowledge of the Zionist Federation.

Yours sincerely,

Arthur James Balfour

Though seriously challenged, 30 years later the Balfour sug-gestion became an acquisition plan covering eastern Galilee, the Upper Jordan Valley, the Negev, and the coastal plain was made. And a suggestion to create an international zone in the city of Jeru-salem was added. The thought of implementing such a plan brought about serious clashes between the Jews and Arabs throughout the Middle East. Though extremely controversial, in 1948, Israel was recognized by the United Nations as a country. Israel was expected to abide by a General Assembly resolution giving Palestinian refu-gees living there, either the right to return and live peaceably, or receive compensation for any abandoned property. Though recog-nized as a country, more clashes ensued and in 1948 the mayhem grew into an all-out war. Life in Palestine stabilized, but friction remained. A barbed-wire fence was constructed separating East Jerusalem from West Jerusalem.

The 1967 Six-Day War

Chafing between neighboring Arabs and the Jewish citizenry reached a crescendo in 1967. Israeli intelligence became aware of a war plan to attack their country. Knowing this, military forces in Israel surprised the United Arab Republic with a preemptive aerial attack of their own.

The Israeli Air Force destroyed an entirely grounded Egyp-tian Air Force. In addition to Egypt, Israel poked Syria and Jordan in the eye by attacking the West Bank, the Gaza Strip, the Sinai Peninsula, and the Golan Heights. During what became known as the Six-Day War, Israeli forces stormed Arab controlled East Jerusalem. They tore down the barbed-wire fence separating East Jerusalem from West Jerusalem and sprinted to the sacred Western Wall. That portion of the wall had spiritual significance because it was part of the once prodigious Herod's Temple. After capturing that part of Old Jerusalem, the Jews claimed it as a reunification, unofficially annexing it to the state of Israel.

Dry Bones

The restoration of a Jewish state in the land of ancient Canaan is one of the most anticipated prophecies in the Bible. God asked in Ezekiel in Chapter 37:1-14, "*Son of man, can these dry bones live? Ezekiel told God, "You know." Then God said to him, "Prophesy to these bones, and say to them, Oh dry bones hear the word of the Lord!" This is what the Sovereign Lord says to these bones: I will make breath enter you, and you will come to life. I will attach tendons to you and make flesh come upon you and cover you with skin; I will put breath in you, and you will come to life. Then you will know that I am the Lord. So I prophesied as I was commanded. And as I was prophesying, there was a noise, a rattling sound, and the bones came together, bone to bone. I looked, and tendons and flesh appeared on them and skin covered them, but there was no breath in them.*" Ezekiel 37:5-8

Conjecturing, but one dimension of this ancient prophesy may have taken place in 1948. With the establishment of Israeli as a recognizable nation, the "dry bones" came together. In 1948, Israel received "tendons, flesh, and skin," but as yet, "no breath." Why? Because the Jewish people still remain under the Mosaic Covenant. At Jesus' Second Advent, the Holy Spirit will come upon the nation of Israel and then the second part of Ezekiel's prophetic words will be fulfilled.

"Then he said to me, 'Prophesy to the breath; prophesy, son of man, and say to it, 'this is what the Sovereign Lord says: Come, breath, from the four winds and breathe into these slain, that they may live.' So I prophesied as he commanded me, and breath entered them; they came to life and stood up on their feet—a vast army. Then he said to me: 'Son of man, these bones are the people of Israel. They say, 'Our bones are dried up and our hope is gone; we are cut off.' Therefore prophesy and say to them: 'this is what the Sovereign Lord says: My people, I am going to open your graves and bring you up from them; I will bring you back to the land of Israel. Then you, my people, will know that I am the Lord, when I open your graves and bring you up from them. I will put my Spirit in you and you will live, and I will settle you in your own land. Then you will know that I the LORD have spoken, and I have done it, declares the Lord." Ezekiel 37:9-14

On a day, known only by God, Jesus will return to earth and God's Holy Spirit will breathe on the Jewish nation. Then, together with all the saints, they will rule and reign with Jesus over the earth for a preordained period of time.

Revival

Psalm 85:6 reads, *"Will you not revive us again, that your people may rejoice in you?"* David's expression of revival suggests an image of spring after a long winter and this condition is the hope of today's church. Without keeping God's Word, the influences of the Holy Spirit have been withheld from the body of Christ. However, with repentance and fervent prayers, the joy found in a spiritual awakening is forthcoming.

Daniel 9:3-19 records a powerful prayer of repentance. Daniel acknowledges in verse four that God is the one who keeps covenant and shows mercy on those who love him and keep his commandments. However, to inherit the promises found in the Covenant of Redemption, people need to hear the Gospel. And then by faith, believe in Jesus' work on the cross, and be baptized in their hearts.

When the Holy Spirit moves mightily across the waters, spiritual revival always manifests itself. However, before a spiritual revival can take place, repentance is imperative. Without question, society has turned its back on God and a spiritual revival is vital to stop society's depth of depravation. Standards of godliness should never be compromised for the sake of offending a society whose morality condones behavior that is biblically ungodly. In the following verses from chapter nine, Daniel's words of repentance serve as an example for today's Christian church to emulate.

"*So I turned to the Lord God and pleaded with him in prayer and petition, in fasting, and in sackcloth and ashes. I prayed to the Lord my God and confessed: Lord, the great and awesome God, who keeps his covenant of love with those who love him and keep his commandments, we have sinned and done wrong. We have been wicked and have rebelled; we have turned away from your commands and laws. We have not listened to your servants the prophets, who spoke in your name to our kings, our princes and our ancestors, and to all the people of the land. Lord, you are righteous, but this day we are covered with shame—the people of Judah and the inhabitants of Jerusalem and all Israel, both near and far, in all the countries where you have scattered us because of our unfaithfulness to you. We and our kings, our princes and our ancestors are covered with shame, Lord because we have sinned against you. The Lord our God is merciful and forgiving, even though we have rebelled against him; we have not obeyed the Lord our God or kept the laws he gave us through his servants the prophets. All Israel has transgressed your law and turned away, refusing to obey you. Therefore the curses and sworn judgments written in the Law of Moses, the servant of God, have been poured out on us, because we have sinned against you. You have fulfilled the words spoken against us and against our rulers by bringing on us great disaster. Under the whole heaven nothing has ever been done like what has been done to Jerusalem. Just as it is written in the Law of Moses, all this disaster has come on us, yet we have not sought the favor of the Lord our God by turning from our sins and giving attention to your truth. The Lord did not hesitate to bring the disaster on us, for the Lord our God is righteous in everything he does;*

yet we have not obeyed him. Now, Lord our God, who brought your people out of Egypt with a mighty hand and who made for yourself a name that endures to this day, we have sinned, we have done wrong. Lord, in keeping with all your righteous acts, turn away your anger and your wrath from Jerusalem, your city, your holy hill. Our sins and the iniquities of our ancestors have made Jerusalem and your people an object of scorn to all those around us. Now, our God, hear the prayers and petitions of your servant. For your sake, Lord, look with favor on your desolate sanctuary. Give ear, our God, and hear; open your eyes and see the desolation of the city that bears your Name. We do not make requests of you because we are righteous, but because of your great mercy. Lord, listen! Lord, forgive! Lord, hear and act! For your sake, my God, do not delay, because your city and your people bear your Name."

THE COVENANT
OF GRACE
AND
JESUS' MISSION
MANDATE

CHAPTER 15

THE NEW COVENANT CHURCH

In the New Testament, Jesus made a strong covenant statement to Peter. In Matthew 16:15-19, Jesus asked Peter directly, *"Who do you say that I am?"* And Peter answered, *"You are the Christ, the Son of the living God."* Jesus praised Peter's response, telling him that upon his revelation, that Jesus was in deed the Christ, the Son of the Living God, *"I will build MY church, and the gates of hell will not prevail against it."* With emphasis on the word *MY*, Jesus stands alone as the architect and owner of the church.

As prophesied, on the Day of Pentecost, the disciples were baptized in the Holy Spirit and the body of Christ, His church, was given birth. Peter came to understand that Christ's church would be made of "living stones." As it reads in 1 Peter 2:5, *"You also, like living stones, are being built into a spiritual house to be a holy priesthood, offering spiritual sacrifices acceptable to God through Jesus Christ."* Then Peter goes on to identify Jesus Christ as its chief cornerstone.

Ezekiel Saw That Day

The Lord revealed to Ezekiel the work of the Holy Spirit. As the link to God's covenant with Jesus, Ezekiel foretold of the Holy Spirit residing within the believer. In Ezekiel 36:25-29, we read, *"I will sprinkle clean water on you, and you will be clean; I will cleanse you from all your impurities and from all your idols. I will give you a new heart and put a new spirit in you; I will remove from you your heart of stone and give you a heart of flesh. And I will put my Spirit in you and move you to follow my decrees and be careful to keep my laws. Then you will live in the land I gave your ancestors; you will be my people, and I will be your God. I will save you from all your uncleanness. I will call for the grain and make it plentiful and will not bring famine upon you."*

It is the Holy Spirit dwelling in one's heart that makes Jesus' command to love one another possible. The Apostle Paul writes clearly in Romans 8:9, *"But you are not in the flesh but in the Spirit, if indeed the Spirit of God dwells in you. Now if anyone does not have the Spirit of Christ, he is not His."* Through the Holy Spirit, God touches us and lets us know how much we are loved.

The Holy Spirit

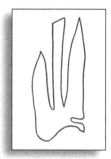

Symbol of the Descending Holy Spirit

In Jeremiah 31:33-34, God made an oath declaring His new covenant taking root in the hearts of men. *"This is the covenant I will make with the people of Israel after that time. I will put my law in their minds and write it on their hearts. I will be their God, and they will be my people. No longer will they teach their neighbor, or say to one another, 'Know the LORD,' because they will all know me, from the least of them to the greatest. For I will forgive their wickedness and will remember their sins no more."* This covenant oath by God was first fulfilled on the day of Pentecost, with more to come.

Evangelist Malcom Smith writes in his book, *The Power of the Blood Covenant*, "It is the quantum leap between knowing about a position in Christ, our representative, and actually experiencing the covenant in the bear hug of God's Spirit." This intense union with the Triune God is described throughout the book of John, Chapters 14 and 15. Apart from the Holy Spirit this new covenant isn't possible. The Holy Spirit serves as a constant reminder, bearing witness and testifying to God's covenant through the blood of His Son. The anointing of the Holy Spirit follows the application of Jesus' blood to our sin, taking us into the very presence of the Father.

As New Testament believers, God does more than dwell with us, He dwells within us. As identified in I Corinthians 3:16 and 6:19, Christians become the privileged tabernacle of God. *"Don't you know that you yourselves are God's temple and that God's Spirit dwells in your midst? Do you not know that your bodies are temples of the Holy Spirit, who is in you, whom you have received from God? You are not your own."* The risen Lord gave this authority to His disciples, and subsequently to all believers, to live in the power of the Holy Spirit. It is an awesome thing knowing that God's majestic power is ready to be unleashed inside covenant people today. As the Spirit begins to move mightily across the waters, revival is forthcoming.

CHAPTER 16

REACHING OUT TO THE GENTILE WORLD

In Matthew 28:18-19, Jesus gave his disciples this great commission. *"All authority in heaven and on earth has been given to me. Therefore go and make disciples of all nations, baptizing them in the name of the Father and of the Son and of the Holy Spirit."* Jesus' command to reach *"all nations"* brings light into a world of darkness.[1] And after his resurrection, Jesus told his disciples (Acts 1:8) that they would receive power when the Holy Spirit came, and that they were to become His witnesses in Jerusalem, and in Judea and Samaria, and to the ends of the earth. And this evangelistic mandate was challenging because to do so required the disciples to face their prejudices.

---

[1] In days past, lamplighters were employed to ignite gas street lights. A story is told about a young Robert Louis Stevenson who one night pressed his nose against his bedroom window. While staring inquisitively out the window, his nanny walked by his room. He saw her, turned around, and exclaimed, "Come here and watch. There is a man going down the street punching holes in the darkness." And isn't that what happens when the gospel of Christ is shared?

Jonah's Disobedience

The early disciples and apostles lived in a society that discriminated against Samaritans and Gentiles. Jewish children, members of God's chosen people, were taught that Gentiles were pagans. Jewish boys were circumcised and their belief in superiority was strengthened through their Bar Mitzvahs. The story of Jonah sheds some light on this truth.

Jonah was first missionary mentioned in the Bible. He was a prophet God sent to Nineveh to bear witness to the Gentiles. Jonah didn't have much of a heart for the Gentiles, though. He resented being sent there and deliberately disobeyed God's instructions by abandoning his assignment. Jonah was afraid that if he went there and was successful, God would show them mercy. But in Jonah's heart, he had rejected the Ninevites, and that was that! He decided to ship himself across the Mediterranean to Tarshish, Spain. He wanted to put as much distance as he could get between himself and the Assyrian city of Nineveh.

While onboard the ship destined for Tarshish, God caused a great wind that put the ship in peril. It wasn't an ordinary storm. Sailors were used to storms. This was an extreme storm, and the sailors aboard were afraid. Capsizing would bring loss of life, cargo, personal possessions, and the ship's crews' livelihood. The sailors suspected divine anger was being hurled at them and Jonah confessed that the storm was his fault. He asked to be tossed overboard, so the crew threw Jonah overboard and the storm subsided. While Jonah was drowning in the sea God sent a whale to rescue him. Three days later the whale belched him out near dry land. After being saved from the sea, Jonah made it to Nineveh and a great revival took place.

An Attitude of Discrimination

During Jesus' time the same prejudice Jonah had, persisted with the disciples. To change their attitude, Jesus intentionally associated with those whom his disciples discriminated against. These encounters undoubtedly made his disciples scratch their heads.

A Roman Centurion

On one occasion Jesus conversed with a Roman centurion. The Roman soldier came to Jesus, asking Him to heal a very sick servant of his. The centurion told Jesus he was a man with authority. And if he just said the words, his subordinates would obey and do as instructed. He knew Jesus was a man of authority, and if Jesus just said the words, his servant would be healed. Jesus complimented the uncircumcised Roman by saying, *"I tell you the truth, I have not found anyone in Israel with such great faith."* By complimenting the soldier, Jesus was announcing to his disciples that His kingdom was far-reaching. Jesus' actions identified that existing in the Gentile world were people of faith worthy of God's grace.

A Canaanite Woman

Then there was a Canaanite woman, begging Jesus to show mercy on her demon-possessed daughter. She cried, "Lord, help me!" Initially Jesus ignored her plea. The disciples were probably pleased that he dismissed her. After all, she was a dirty Gentile and a second-class Canaanite women. For a Jewish rabbi to stop and converse with a Canaanite woman was culturally unacceptable. But the woman persisted and Jesus stopped to talk with her. Jesus told her that it wasn't right to take food away from God's chosen people. She humbly replied, *"Yes Lord, but even the dogs eat the crumbs that fall from their master's table."* Jesus was touched by her response and said to her, *"Woman, you have great faith! Your request is granted."* As the disciples witnessed the interaction, they probably wondered to themselves, "Why in the world would Jesus interact with someone like her?" They never realized that Jesus was evangelizing to *"all people"* and *"all nations."*

A Promiscuous Samaritan Woman

In the fourth chapter of John, we read where Jesus intentionally passed through Samaria. He had a divine encounter with a promiscuous woman. She was at a well, not looking for Jesus, but Jesus came to meet up with her. She came to draw water out of the well in the heat of the day. Jesus was observing her and said, *"Will you give me a drink?"* The Samaritan woman responded, *"You are a Jew and I am a Samaritan woman. How can you ask me for a drink?"* Jesus answered her, *"If you knew the gift of God and who it is that asks you for a drink, you would have asked him and he would have given you living water."* *"Sir, you have nothing to draw with and the well is deep. Where can you get this living water? Are you greater than our father Jacob, who gave us the well and drank from it himself, as did also his sons and his livestock?"* Jesus answered, *"Everyone who drinks this water will be thirsty again, but whoever drinks the water I give them will never thirst. Indeed, the water I give them will become in them a spring of water welling up to eternal life."* The woman said to him, *"Sir, give me this water so that I won't get thirsty and have to keep coming here to draw water."* He told her, *"Go, call your husband and come back." "I have no husband,"* she replied. Jesus said to her, *"You are right when you say you have no husband. The fact is, you have had five husbands, and the man you now have is not your husband. What you have just said is quite true." "Sir, I can see that you are a prophet. Our ancestors worshiped on this mountain, but you Jews claim that the place where we must worship is in Jerusalem." "Woman,"* Jesus replied, *"believe me, a time is coming when you will worship the Father neither on this mountain nor in Jerusalem. You Samaritans worship what you do not know; we worship what we do know, for salvation is from the Jews. Yet a time is coming and has now come when the true worshipers will worship the Father in the Spirit and in truth, for they are the kind of worshipers the Father seeks. God is spirit, and his worshipers must worship in the Spirit and in truth."* The woman said, *"I know that Messiah is coming. When he comes, he will explain everything to us."* Then Jesus declared, *"I, the one speaking to you—I am he."* Just then his disciples returned and were surprised to find him talking with a woman. But no one asked, *"Why are you talking with her?"* However, they must have wondered because talking with this Samaritan[2] women was a cultural faux pas. But to Jesus, His reputation wasn't in question. Traditional prejudices and segregation meant nothing to Him. Jesus brought the gospel to her and she received Jesus as her Lord. She went back to her town and witnessed to others who also believed. By example Jesus was validating that everyone was invited to receive God's grace and salvation.

The Good Samaritan

What defined Jesus was his universal compassion. And His depth of compassion overcame prejudicial customs. Jesus conveyed this principle of compassion in a story about the Good Samaritan. When the disciples listened to the story, it must have challenged the very core of their thinking.

Jesus told of a man beaten and left for dead by the side of a road. By chance, a priest came by and when he saw the man, crossed over to the other side. Then a religious Levite came by, and after seeing the man in his beaten condition, passed over to the other side of the road, too. But then a lowly Samaritan came

---

[2] The Samaritans occupied the hill country of Israel. When Israel was taken captive by the Assyrian army in 723 B.C., members of the Assyrians stayed behind to inhabit the land. The pagan foreigners introduced their idolatry and influenced a religion in Samaria that became a mixture of Judaism and idolatry. Around 538 B.C., non-idol worshipping Samaritans chose as their sacred place of worship, Mt. Gerizim. On this mountain they believed father Abraham sacrificed Isaac. Their belief overrode the rival belief of Mt. Moriah in Jerusalem and it never sat well with the Jews in Jerusalem. The rivalry became contentious as the Samaritans were held in contempt. In this passage, the Samaritan woman could have taken offense to Jesus' statement about her religion, but instead she went and brought back the whole town to hear more of Jesus' teachings. Jesus stayed for two days and during his time of teaching, many believed that He was indeed the Savior of the world.

by who looked upon the man with compassion. The Samaritan seized the opportunity to show the man mercy and unconditional love. He came to his aid and cared for him. Then Jesus asked, *"Which of these three men do you think was a neighbor to the man who fell into the hands of the robbers?"* Luke 10:36

The Vision that Changed Peter's Attitude

The disciples and apostles initially confined their witness to Jewish acquaintances and circumcised converts. To the early disciples, the uncircumcised could not enter the kingdom of God. And this prejudice blinded them from spreading the *"good news"* to *"all nations."* Being a devout Jew, Jesus' inclusive mandate was difficult for Peter to comprehend. To help him better understand all-inclusiveness, God revealed to Peter, in a vision, that *"all nations"* included the Gentile world. The revelation to Peter is found in the book of Acts, chapters 10 and 11.

Cornelius Calls for Peter

Peter's revelation took place in the northcentral Israeli town of Caesarea, a port city located midway between Tel Aviv and Haifa. In Caesarea, there lived an uncircumcised Roman centurion named Cornelius. He was there with an Italian regiment on assignment. The Bible tells us he and all his family were devout and God-fearing. He gave generously to those in need and prayed regularly to God. Though a Gentile, he had great faith and recognized the God of the Jews.

One day, around 3:00 in the afternoon, an angel on assignment visited Cornelius. The angel called Cornelius by name and revealed to him that his prayers and gifts to the poor had been recognized by God. His earnest seeking made Cornelius an aspirant to receive the light of the Gospel and the gift of salvation. He was told to send some men to Joppa and bring back a certain man named Simon, called Peter. And he could be found staying in the home of Simon the Tanner. Joppa was a Mediterranean port city located 40 miles south of Caesarea. After the angel left, Cornelius did as he was instructed. Cornelius arranged for two regular servants and a devout soldier of his to make the journey to Joppa.

Peter's Trance

The next day, around noon, Peter went up to pray on the roof of the house where he was staying. After reaching the roof, he found himself hungry. He asked that some food be prepared and brought to him. While waiting for the food, Peter fell into an induced trance. He saw heaven open up and something like a large net lowered to earth by its four corners. Inside the lowered net were animals forbidden by the Hebrew law to be eaten, including camels, pigs, rabbits, reptiles and certain scavenger birds. Then a voice rang out, *"Get up Peter. Kill and eat."* Peter said, *"Surely not, Lord. I've never eaten anything impure or unclean."* Jewish law forbade the Hebrew people from eating the animals captured in the net. Peter's mind was confused. Focusing on the forbidden passages found in Leviticus 11:4-27 and Deuteronomy 14:3-20, he must have asked himself, "Why am I being told that eating these unclean and impure animals is okay now?" Then God's voice said, ***"Don't call anything impure that God has made clean."*** This happened three times and then the net was taken back into heaven. Peter knew it was Lord's voice, and being outranked, Peter was ready to do as commanded. Something was up, but what?

While contemplating the meaning of the vision, the men sent by Cornelius showed up at Simon the Tanner's house. The men inquired if Simon Peter was present. Upstairs the Holy Spirit was simultaneously prompting Peter. He was told that downstairs three men, sent by God, were inquiring about him. He was to go downstairs, meet with them, and then go with them. Peter went downstairs and acknowledged that he was the person for whom they were looking. He queried why they sought him. The men told him that a Roman centurion named Cornelius had sent them. He was a righteous and God-fearing man, respected by the Jewish citizenry. And that a holy angel had visited with Cornelius, advising him to send men to Joppa and ask for Peter. They said, ***"Cornelius wants you to come to his house and speak with him."*** After listening to them, Peter invited the men into the house as his guests. They shared a meal and stayed the night.

Explanation of Peter's Vision

Peter's vision was an object lesson. When the heavens opened, dropping the net out of the sky, a mystery was unfolding. It was the revelation of God's grace, allowing "all people" to receive the gift of salvation. The great net with its four corners was emblematic of the entire world and its myriad of nations. The Gospel was to be preached to the four corners of the world, offering its blessings to all inhabitants, without distinction of ethnicity, nationality, etc.

This vision revealed to Peter that the forbidden dietary rituals found in the Torah were to be challenged. With Jesus' resurrection, a new era was ushered in, and believers were not to call unclean what God had made clean. In essence, if God chose to cleanse a person, regardless of that person's ethnicity, nationality, or religious affiliation, that person must be received as a spiritual brother or sister. By biblical standards as written in Deuteronomy 19:15, all testimony and evidence had to be confirmed by two or three witnesses. To satisfy that requirement, Peter's vision was repeated three times. Peter came to understand, by the work of the Holy Spirit, that Cornelius represented the Gentile world, a world formerly considered unclean by the Jewish people. It was definably a turning point in Peter's ministry and a major step toward world evangelism. In this biblical story, an action taken by Peter showed evidence of Peter's understanding. He did something that was highly unusual. Peter invited the three Gentile men into his quarters to break bread and spend the night. Without an understanding of God's desire, his prejudice would have kept them outside of his living quarters.

Peter Visits the House of Cornelius

The next morning, Peter and six of his Christian believers, plus the men sent by Cornelius, left on a two day journey through the Plain of Sharon to Caesarea. As they trekked north near the aqua-colored Mediterranean Sea, it would have resembled a caravan. Once they arrived in Caesarea, Cornelius welcomed Peter, bowing down before him. Apparently Cornelius was in awe of the person the angelic being told him to summon. But Peter made him stand up, making it clear to Cornelius that the two of them were on even ground. While dialoguing, Peter discovered a large group of Cornelius' relatives and close friends gathering. Confronting the gathered crowd, Peter spoke the words found in Acts 10:28-29. *"You are well aware that it is against our law (taboo) for a Jew to associate with or visit a Gentile. But God has shown me that I should not call anyone impure or unclean. So when I was sent for, I came without raising any objection. May I ask why you sent for me?"* Cornelius responded by telling the gathered assembly how an angel in shining clothes appeared to him. The angel said that God had heard his prayers and Cornelius was to send for a person named Simon, called Peter. The angelic being told him that Peter would be in Joppa staying at the home of Simon the Tanner. Looking at Peter, Cornelius continued, *"So I sent for you immediately, and it was good for you to come. Now we are here in the presence of God to listen to everything the Lord has commanded you to tell us."* Cornelius' response indicated that God had arranged this extraordinary meeting.

Peter told the crowd that he realized God wasn't showing any favoritism, but accepts from every nation those who fear him and do what is right. Peter went on to tell them he was an eyewitness to everything Jesus did on earth and shared in an abridged version,

Jesus' life, death, and resurrection. Peter acknowledged that Jesus was Lord of all people. And in so many words, Peter clarified that though God doesn't show favoritism with nations, he does make distinctions about religion. Only those who worship the one true God, and His Son, Jesus Christ, can have eternal life. Peter's mission to Caesarea bears witness that those who earnestly seek God are rewarded with His presence.

While Peter was still speaking, the Holy Spirit fell upon those present in the room. Those traveling with Peter to Caesarea were astonished. As Hebrew converts, they were circumcised, but these Gentiles were not. Listening to the Gentiles speak in tongues and praising God seemed implausible. Yet it was happening and they were witnesses. The work of the Holy Spirit was an epiphany for Peter. He suggested baptizing the new converts with water, and in the name of Jesus Christ and ordered it to be done.

At the foot of the cross, the playing field is level. As Christians we serve an impartial God who sent a universal Jesus to save all of us from our sins. This unmeasurable act of love was truly a reflection of God's amazing grace.

Romans 10:12-13 tells us, *"For there is no difference between Jew and Gentile, the same Lord is Lord of all and richly blesses all who call on him, for, everyone who calls on the name of the Lord will be saved."*

CHAPTER 17

REACHING ALL NATIONS

In Genesis 22:18, the Lord made this profound statement to Abram, *"In your seed all the nations will be blessed because you obeyed my voice."* The Apostle Paul wrote in Galatians 3:16, *"Now to Abraham and his seed were the promises made. He does not say, 'and to seeds,' as of many, but as of one, 'and to your Seed,' who is Christ."* And with the advent of Jesus, *"all nations were blessed."* By Jesus' work on the cross, the whole world was blessed. The Israelites were to be God's light to the nations, manifesting God's love, provision and protection. By witnessing God's caring for them, the other nations received an implied invitation to call upon their God. But now God's invitation was overt. Jesus sent his disciples to share the gospel of grace to the nations.

The Council at Jerusalem

As found in Acts 15:28-29, during the Council at Jerusalem, Peter, Barnabas, Paul and James had to convince the early disciples that the Holy Spirit had been shared with the culturally different Gentiles. Peter and Paul addressed the gathering and told them that salvation was the issue not cultural purity. It was to be understood that the Gentiles were not to be subjected to Jewish traditions. However, everyone who turned to God was expected to follow the precepts set forth by Jesus. By revealing what had taken place at the home of Cornelius, the skeptical disciples at the conference bought-in to the idea of cultural diversity. The evidence of their acceptance was in letter sent by the body of disciples to the new believers in Antioch which read, *"It seemed good to the Holy Spirit and to us not to burden you with anything beyond the following requirements: You are to abstain from food sacrificed to idols, from blood, from the meat of strangled animals and from sexual immorality. You will do well to avoid these things."* The disciples' acceptance of this principle opened the door to evangelize *"all nations."* Had their argument been lost, many "splinter-groups" of Judaism may have been created.

The Apostle Paul

Paul understood that salvation was something apart from Jewish law and tradition; it was achieved by faith in Jesus Christ. And that the gospel of grace was for all people, both Jew and Gentile. As stated earlier, in the beginning, Jewish Christians expected converts to be circumcised. To clear up this misunderstanding, Paul wrote in I Corinthians 9:19-22, *"though I am free and belong to no one, I have made myself a slave to everyone, to win as many as possible. To the Jews I became like a Jew, to win the Jews. To those under the law I became like one under the law (though I myself am not under the law), so as to win those under the law. To those not having the law I became like one not having the law (though I am not free from God's law but am under Christ's law), so as to win those not having the law. To the weak I became weak, to win the weak. I have become all things to all people so that by all possible means I might save some."* This was a powerful revelation and the beginning of contextualization.

Hudson Taylor

An example of contextualization is found in the behavior of a British missionary named Hudson Taylor. In the 1800's, Hudson was sent to evangelize Shanghai, China. Instead of preserving his traditional British style of dress, Taylor felt that the Gospel would take root more easily if he and his missionary partners affirmed the Chinese culture. So while in Shanghai, he and his group wore their hair like the Chinese and donned their style of dress. In brief, when the Chinese culture wasn't contrary to the Gospel, Hudson embraced the tradition. Taylor affirmed Apostle Paul's epiphany when he said, "Let us in everything not sinful become like the Chinese, that by all means we may save some."

Cultural Immersion

Without having a clear understanding of cultural differences, inadvertently, hindrances are tossed in the pathway of accepting the Gospel. Too often, unbiblical religious traditions and cultural hang-ups become road-blocks to effective evangelism. Superficial matters shouldn't be allowed to impede the opportunity to receive the gospel of forgiveness and salvation through Jesus Christ. It is the responsibility of all missionaries to develop friendships that are strong enough to bear the weight of God's truth. And to do so often requires adopting some cultural observances.

Cultural values produce ethnic-pride and are essential behaviors in a nation's heritage. Before asking others to commit cultural suicide, it is best to sort out what is important, and what is not. A modern example is an organization founded in 1973 called *Jews for Jesus.*

Members of this group are Jews who embrace Christian theology, professing Yeshua (Jesus) as their Lord and Savior, while simultaneously retaining their Hebrew culture. Sometimes referred to as Messianic Jews, these Christian Jews celebrate Passover, Rosh Hashanah, and Yom Kippur. They continue to circumcise their male babies at birth, observe the Sabbath beginning at sundown on Friday, conduct Bar and Bat Mitzvahs, and observe kosher dietary laws. While holding on to their rich covenant heritage, they embrace the fullness of God's grace and mercy in Jesus Christ, integrating traditional culture with solid Christian doctrine.

EPILOGUE

God's Covenant Invitation

Jesus' blood was, and is, the only sacrifice accepted by God to completely atone for man's sins. No offering of any other kind will work. Forgiveness of sin can't be achieved by any other substitutionary offering, including works. It is obtained solely by faith in God's Covenant of Redemption. God's precious gift is described Ephesians 2:4-10. *"But because of his great love for us, God, who is rich in mercy, made us alive with Christ even when we were dead in transgressions—it is by grace you have been saved. And God raised us up with Christ and seated us with him in the heavenly realms in Christ Jesus, in order that in the coming ages he might show the incomparable riches of his grace, expressed in his kindness to us in Christ Jesus. For it is by grace you have been saved, through faith—and this is not from yourselves, it is the gift of God—not by works, so that no one can boast. For we are God's handiwork, created in Christ Jesus to do good works, which God prepared in advance for us to do."*

So what must a person believe to achieve covenant status with God? By faith, a person must believe that Jesus' sacrificed blood on the cross at Calvary compensated for their sins. The Apostle Paul explains in II Corinthians 3:17-18 that when a person accepts Christ as their personal savior, they are transformed. Their previous image, defaced by sin, is gradually restored into the divine image of Christ, *"from glory to glory."* But how does this happen?

Jesus was immersed in the Jordan River by John the Baptist. Symbolically, Jesus drowned under the water. When he came up out of the water, he was renewed by the presence of the Holy Spirit. When Jesus rose from the grave, he figuratively came up out of the water and to give eternal life to all believers. So what must one do to receive this gift of eternal life? It begins through spiritual baptism. Spiritual baptism takes place at the moment one accepts Jesus as his or her personal savior. Because at that moment, the indwelling of God's Holy Spirit declares that through the blood sacrifice of Christ, he or she is now in covenant with the Father and, as such, a partaker in God's plan for divine amnesty. Through the miracle of grace, the unrighteous become righteous. We know from I John 1:9, *"If we confess our sins, he is faithful and just and will forgive us our sins and purify us from all unrighteousness."*

Spiritual baptism is often celebrated through ceremonial water baptism. In baptism, a believer's unholy covenant with sin is renounced openly. Through immersion the old nature is drowned and coming up out of the water is representational of resurrecting into a new life with Christ. The Holy Spirit restores one's heart, empowers you to resist temptation by implanting a strong desire to please God.

When a person accepts Jesus Christ as his or her personal Savior, they enter into an everlasting blood covenant. II Corinthians 5:21 assures all followers of Christ that Jesus' righteousness has been imputed to them. *"God made him who had no sin to be sin for us, so that in him we might become the righteousness of God."* And when he or she receives the Holy Spirit, they become sealed in the Father's blood covenant with His Son. Ephesians 1:13 tells us, *"And you also were included in Christ when you heard the message of truth, the gospel of your salvation. When you believed, you were marked in him with a seal, the promised Holy Spirit."* John 1:7 reminds us that *"if we walk in the light, as he is in the light, we have fellowship with one another, and the blood of Jesus, his Son, purifies us from all sin."* Again, the marvelous truth of God's everlasting covenant is reiterated by the Apostle Paul in Romans 8:37-38. *"For I am convinced that neither death nor life, neither angels nor demons, neither the present nor the future, nor any powers, neither height nor depth, nor anything else in all creation, will be able to separate us from the love of God that is in Christ Jesus our Lord."*

The New Testament covenant assures us that one day all believers are going to be with Jesus. In John 14:3 Jesus said *"And if I go and prepare a place for you, I will come back and take you to be with me that you also may be where I am."* What a blessed thought.

Now that you have read about God as the divine covenant maker and covenant keeper, an open invitation is extended for those desiring to enter into a blood covenant with Him. John 3:16 (KJV) reminds us, *"For God so loved the world, that he gave his only begotten Son, that whosoever believeth in him should not perish, but have everlasting life."* Being a "whosoever" doesn't discriminate against anyone. So God's invitation remains wide open.

Abba, Father

Very carefully read these verses from Romans 8:14-16 (KJV). *"For as many as are led by the Spirit of God, they are the sons of God. For ye have not received the spirit of bondage again to fear; but ye have received the Spirit of adoption, whereby we cry, Abba, Father. The Spirit itself bears witness with our spirit, that we are the children of God."* This passage reveals a very special relationship to God; that of adopted children. Children who have become joint-heirs in the glory of Christ Jesus. By the workings of the Holy Spirit, the relationship once reserved for the Israelites has become available to all spiritual Israelites, regardless of nationality or ethnicity.

In the Middle East, not every son has the right to use the expression, "Abba, Father." Only the favorite son has that privilege. While growing up in Egypt, author Mike Ahmed was the favored son in his family. He was privileged to use the expression, while his siblings were required to use the expressions of dad, father, or sir. He alone was allowed to say, "Abba, Father." In addition, as the favored son, he had privileged access to his father's time, wealth, and friends. For example, if an Egyptian father was having a conversation with a covenant friend, and a non-privileged child interrupted, the covenant partner would have authority to discipline the child for interrupting. However, should a favorite one interrupt, only the father would have the right to discipline. Understanding this cultural manner has a spiritual application, too. Should the devil ever attempt to discipline, shame, or accuse God's elect over an unrighteous behavior, a Christian's cry should be, "Abba Father." The expression elevates the Christian to his or her superior position. As a child of God, never make agreement with the devil. The Apostle Paul reminds Christians that they have received the Spirit of adoption, and therefore cry, "Abba Father." Always remember, God forgives confessed sin and the Holy Spirit, as every Christian's advocate, stands in to deride the accuser's ploy.

Restoration

In a covenant culture, a breach is sometimes restored by each party feeding the other bread. Non-verbally, they are saying to each other, "I am back in you again and everything between us is restored." And isn't that what Jesus taught his disciples during their first communion? *"I put myself inside you and I will dwell there forever. This is my blood, the blood of the New Covenant."*

Romans 8:15 tells us, *"The Spirit you received does not make you slaves, so that you live in fear again; rather, the Spirit you received brought about your adoption to sonship. And by him we* cry, 'Abba, Father.' " Our Father's great love and mercy is demonstrated even further in Daniel 9:9. In this verse we read, *"The Lord our God is merciful and forgiving, even though we have rebelled against him."* This passage reminds us that we don't make requests to the Lord because we are righteous, but because God shows us great mercy. Isn't that astounding? The God of Creation knows us, loves us, and desires to hear our prayers in order to show us mercy.

What a privilege it is to be in covenant with God through Christ Jesus. By faith, Christ dwells in a believer's heart and all of His righteousness is credited to them. Through communion, believers are reminded of Christ's body and blood residing within them, giving them authority to cry, "Abba Father." Christians must never forget that they belong to God through Christ Jesus. We are his adopted children. *"You, dear children, are from God and have overcome them, because the one who is in you is greater than the one who is in the world."* I John 4:4

Jesus says in Revelation 3:20, *"Here I am! I stand at the door and knock. If anyone hears my voice and opens the door, I will come in and eat with that person, and they with me."* So if you have not already accepted His invitation, but desire to do so, here is what to do:

- Obtain a loaf of bread and raise it up to God.

- Take a piece of that bread and eat it as part of your covenant meal with Jesus.

- To complete the covenant meal, drink some wine or grape juice.

- During your meal with God, confess your sinful nature and ask for forgiveness. By doing this you will become a favored child of God.

- Then look for a Bible-believing church to attend and ask to be baptized with water. Once you are baptized, ask God's Holy Spirit to come and live inside of you. The Holy Spirit will guide you in all truth and you will become a new creation.

The Bible assures us that old things will pass away and your life will begin anew. Romans 8:15 tells us, *"The Spirit you received does not make you slaves, so that you live in fear again; rather, the Spirit you received brought about your adoption to sonship. And by him we cry, 'Abba, Father.'"*

Now may the Lord of Heaven be with you today, tomorrow and forever. Amen.

91392443R00134

Made in the USA
Columbia, SC
20 March 2018